Super Smoothies

Celine Tregan

Super Smoothies
Celine Tregan

Photographer: Antoine Sicotte
Cover photo: Melanie Bellemare
Graphic designers: Karine Lacroix,
Laurie Auger and Gabrielle Godbout
Cover designer: Karine Lacroix
Food stylist: Veronique Paradis
English translators: Patricia Boushel and
Lorien Jones
Copy editor: Anna Phelan

ISBN: 978-2-920943-77-3

©2014, Cardinal Publishing Group/
Les Éditions Cardinal
www.cardinalpublishinggroup.com
All rights reserved.

Legal deposit: 2014
Library and Archives Canada
Bibliothèque et Archives Nationales du Québec
ISBN: 978-2-920943-77-3

We acknowledge the financial support
of the Government of Canada through
the Book Publishing Industry Development
Program (BPIDP) for our publishing activities
and the support of the Government of Quebec
through the tax credits for book publishing
program – SODEC.

Printed in Canada

Super Smoothies

Celine Tregan

145 delicious
smoothies to improve
your health

cardinal

Table of Contents

Warning

The History of Smoothies

A smoothie is a thick beverage made from fresh fruit and/or vegetables, rich in vitamins and mineral nutrients, often blended with dairy products, soy milk, or crushed ice, to which various supplements like vitamins, protein, ginseng, spirulina, lecithin, etc. can be added. The smoothie was invented in California in 1960 by Stephen Kuhnau, who based his lower-calorie creation on the traditional milkshake. Kuhnau wanted to offer a similar beverage to individuals with cow's milk allergies and health-conscious people seeking a simple, natural alternative. His original recipes are made with fruit (fresh or frozen) blended with ice, yogurt, or green tea.

Since the 1990s, smoothies have been marketed as a health food, often made with carrots or soy milk as a base and added supplements to compensate for dietary deficiencies. The evolution of tastes, the availability of flavorful ingredients, and the unwavering popularity of the smoothie, along with its general great taste and infinite nutritional benefits, make it simultaneously a delicious beverage, a decadent dessert, an energizing tonic, a tasty snack, an ideal diet food, and a complete meal. A single smoothie can provide almost half of the daily-recommended serving of fruits and vegetables with a delicious flavor that only fresh raw fruits and vegetables can provide, all in one glass.

The ABCs of Successful Smoothies

Here are a few basic guidelines to follow:

Choose fresh, ripe fruits and vegetables.

For the very best blend, choose fruits and vegetables that are in season.

Eat fruit as soon as possible after buying. Over time, fruit will dry out and become less juicy.

Blend the fruit (or vegetable) with the highest water content first. Apples, for example, should be added first, followed by the other fruits and vegetables of your choice.

To ensure that your smoothie is well blended, cut the fruit into equal-sized pieces.

Adding ice makes for a deliciously cold smoothie and gives it a lovely texture, but if it is not consumed immediately, your tasty, vitamin-packed drink will become unpleasantly watered down. Keep crushed ice in the freezer, and always add it at the very end of preparation.

Tip

To prepare the perfect smoothie, always purée ice (at least 5 ice cubes or pieces per serving) along with the juice, which should be added after blending the fruits and/or vegetables.

Smoothies can be stored in the refrigerator for up to 24 hours without oxidizing. Dairy products should only be added immediately before consuming.

Freezing celery, avocado, parsley, and ginger is not recommended.

Before blending, peel the fruits and vegetables and remove any pits or seeds, unless otherwise indicated.

Tip

Crush ice with a blender, if you have one. If not, put ice cubes into a plastic bag and crush with a hard object.

Substitute crushed ice with sorbet, ice cream, or frozen berries (raspberries, strawberries, blueberries, cranberries, etc.).

To thicken a smoothie, add yogurt. If your smoothie is too thick, add filtered water or fruit juice. It is best to start with a small amount of liquid and add more if necessary. Try substituting water with an infusion, a non-dairy milk, fruit kefir, apple juice, or orange juice.

Ideally, a smoothie should contain two or three different types of fruit, but a smoothie made with only one type of fruit will still be delicious! Bananas and avocados give smoothies an even creamier texture. Always choose ripe fruit, and combine complementing fruits (peach/apricot, red fruit, pears and grapefruit, etc.).

The Very Best Ingredients

Choosing Fruit

As a general rule, try to avoid using more than three different fruits in a single smoothie so that you can fully appreciate the flavors of the blend you have chosen. To benefit from all of the vitamins in a piece of fruit, do not peel it before blending, because most of the vitamins are concentrated in the peel. However, it is important to remove the pith on citrus fruits, as it will give your smoothie a bitter taste.

To balance out different textures, use an equal blend of starchy and juicy fruits. If the mixture is too thick, add water. If you want to prepare smoothies with berries that are out of season, consider buying prepackaged frozen fruit, which can be used year-round. Add them, still frozen, directly to the blender and you will not even need to add ice cubes. If possible, freeze berries yourself when they are in season—they will only be more delicious!

The principle behind freezing fruit is simple: choose firm fruit, wash it thoroughly, and dry it well. For stone fruit, remove the pit and place on a baking sheet lined with parchment paper. Freeze the fruit directly on the baking sheet and then transfer it to plastic freezer bags, ideally in smaller amounts and in several portions. Before closing the freezer bags, squeeze out as much air as possible. Write the name of the fruit and the freezing date on the bag.

For berries, it is best not to wash before freezing. Place berries in a single layer on a large baking sheet lined with parchment paper, freeze, and transfer to freezer bags.

Peel fruits like bananas, mangoes, papayas, cantaloupe, and watermelon, and then purée and pour into ice cube trays. Freeze, remove from trays, and transfer to freezer bags for a flavorful, no-fuss addition to your smoothies.

Health Info

Digestive Aids	Stimulating and revitalizing	Relaxing
pineapples	bananas	apricots
cherries	lemons	peaches
lemons	figs	plums
strawberries	rapsberries	prunes
grapefruits	mango	pears
apples	blackberries	grapes
	oranges	

Fruit	Health Benefits

Apricot

The apricot is antianemic, astringent, and stimulates the appetite, and is rich in minerals, helps prevent rickets, and helps fight fatigue and depression. It is high in potassium, is a good source of vitamins C, B1, B2, B5, and PP, and is rich in sugar, mineral nutrients, and many trace elements, which contribute to the fruit's antianemic and antiasthenic properties. The fruit is also extremely rich in beta-carotene, a precursor to vitamin A, which plays an important role in the composition of pigments in the retina, improves nighttime vision, helps protect the skin and mucous membranes, and acts as a natural antioxidant.

Açaí

Açaí is sold as a frozen pulp or as a powdered preparation of freeze-dried extract. The berry improves digestion, provides energy, boosts endurance and brain function, and fights insomnia.

Acerola

The acerola (also known as the Barbados or West Indian cherry) is widely cultivated in Brazil. It is an excellent tonic, stimulates the immune system, and contains minerals and other active ingredients such as beta-carotene, vitamin B3, phosphorus, calcium, iron, etc.

Pineapple

Pineapple is widely appreciated for its characteristic sweet, juicy flesh as well as for its low calorie count and high concentration of vitamins and minerals. It is also high in fiber, potassium, vitamin C, magnesium, and carotene, acts as an antiseptic and an intestinal anti-inflammatory agent, and helps fight arteriosclerosis.

Sea Buckthorn

This plant is very rich in vitamins C, E, A, B1, B2, F, K and P, in proteins (globulin and albumin in particular), saturated fatty acids (palmitic and palmitoleic acids), unsaturated fatty acids (linolenic and linoleic acids), amino acids, sugars, and carbohydrates. The sea buckthorn's fruit has a high concentration of vitamin C—about 30 times greater than oranges, 25 times greater than strawberries, and 5 times greater than kiwis. The pulp is rich in omega-7, a rare and highly beneficial fatty acid found in only two vegetables: the macadamia nut and sea buckthorn.

Avocado

Beneficial to the circulatory system thanks to the oleic acid it contains, the avocado provides energy and is highly nutritious, and is easy to digest despite its high fat content. It is beneficial to the stomach and intestines, and is an excellent source of potassium and folate, a good source of vitamin B6, and contains magnesium, pantothenic acid, vitamin C, copper, niacin, iron, vitamin A, and zinc.

Banana

The banana is highly regarded as a powerful antioxidant thanks to the dopamine it contains, which helps prevent cardiovascular diseases, age-related illnesses, and more. It also reduces the risk of certain cancers, including kidney cancer and colorectal cancer, and the phospholipids and pectin it contains helps prevent the development of ulcers in the stomach's mucous membrane. The banana is also rich in calories, fiber and cramp-fighting potassium, provides energy, and contains water, iron, magnesium, and carbohydrates.

Fruit	Health Benefits
Blueberry	Astringent, antibacterial, and antidiuretic, this berry is recommended in cases of gastroenteritis and cystitis, and to protect blood vessels. A source of vitamin C, potassium, sodium, and fiber, it contains several acids, namely oxalic, maleic, and citric acids.
Cranberry	This astringent berry is beneficial for blood circulation, the skin, and the digestive system. It is used to treat urinary infections and to correct circulatory system deficiencies. Cranberries contain vitamin C and potassium. It is also loaded with various acids, mainly oxalic and citric acids, to which this berry owes its rather tart taste.
Blackcurrant	This berry contains a high amount of complex molecules called anthocyanins, which are recognized as antioxidants given that their main attribute, together with the blackcurrant's other molecules, namely quercetin, is to trap the free radicals responsible for aging. Among the fruits grown in the temperate regions, it has one of the highest concentrations of polyphenols, organic molecules with well-known antioxidant effects.
Cherry	Possessing remineralising, diuretic, antiarthritic, and antirhumatismal properties, this slightly laxative fruit is recognized for its detoxifying virtues. While the sweet cherry is a good source of potassium, the sour cherry is an even higher source.
Lemon	Renowned for its many virtues, this citrus fruit kills bacteria, helps expel intestinal worms, and acts as an antiseptic, an antirheumatic, and a diuretic. It also invigorates and revitalizes. Its essence is comprised of approximately 95% terpenes (terebenthine), making it an effective expectorant, and it is one of the most effective natural antiseptics. Recognized for its high vitamin C content, it also contains potassium and folate.
Date	Ultra-nutritious, remineralizing, and tonifying, dates help renew red blood cells, and dried, they contain a great deal of potassium. Dates are a source of copper, pantothenic acid, vitamin B6, niacin, magnesium and iron.
Fig	Figs contain vitamin B6, sodium, phosphorus, pantothenic acid, riboflavin, zinc, and thiamine. They stimulate lazy intestines and possess diuretic, laxative, and strengthening properties. When fresh, they are nutritious as well as a good source of potassium, magnesium, iron, and copper, and a source of fiber.
Strawberry	This berry contains vitamin C, potassium, folate, pantothenic acid, and magnesium. Thirst-quenching and remineralizing, this little fruit stimulates the system's defenses against infections. It is also known as an effective tonic, purgative, diuretic, and astringent.
Raspberry	The raspberry is a good source of vitamin C, potassium, and magnesium, a high source of fiber, and contains traces of calcium and vitamin A. A natural diuretic, antiasthenic, and heart strengthener, this berry also relieves heartburn and constipation. The raspberry bush's leaves, when infused as a tea, have astringent, diuretic, and laxative properties, and help stimulate menstruation.

Fruit	Health Benefits
Goji (berry)	The Goji berry contains high concentrations of vitamin C and is very rich in antioxidants, elements that help prevent diseases associated with aging, such as cardiovascular disease and cancer.
Guava	Guava is one of the best sources of vitamin C and dietary fiber, containing nearly five times as much as an orange. Guava accelerates the healing of skin lesions and prevents the development of boils. Its fiber inhibits constipation and regulates the bowels. It also helps lower cholesterol levels, acting as a natural aid in the prevention of heart disorders.
Pomegranate	Three times richer in antioxidants than green tea, this red fruit, which resembles the apple, helps fight against cell oxidation and the aging of the skin.
Red Currant	This strengthening berry is often recommended to help slow the onset of osteoporosis. It stimulates the appetite as well as digestion, and acts as a purgative, especially when it is darker in color.
Kiwi	An excellent source of vitamin C and potassium, the kiwi also contains magnesium and traces of phosphorus, iron, and vitamin A. A diuretic, laxative and antiscorbutic, kiwi is recommended in the prevention of cardiovascular issues. It also contains many polyphenols, substances that help fight free radicals. An accumulation of free radicals promotes premature cellular aging and cardiovascular illnesses, as well as certain cancers.
Lychee	High in fiber, lychee fruit helps regulate the appetite. This fruit is actually quite sweet, but extremely refreshing thanks to its high water content. Its principal nutritional asset is its wealth of vitamin C: it contains as much as an orange, a kiwi, or a grapefruit. Lychee also contains vitamin B and numerous minerals and micronutrients. It is a natural pain reliever, and helps relieve stomach pain and promote bowel movements.
Mandarin	This citrus fruit is an excellent source of vitamin C and contains potassium, vitamin A, and folate. A sedative that also protects blood vessels, the mandarin stabilizes hypertension and nervous excitement.
Mangosteen	The mangosteen's flesh is rich in carbohydrates, vitamin C, calcium, magnesium, and potassium. An antioxidant, it fights off fever and treats all kinds of infections while boosting energy and acting as a natural anti-inflammatory. Its skin contains high concentrations of xanthones, a family of unique phytonutrients. Scientists have discovered that, when eaten regularly, the mangosteen contributes to the healthy functioning of the body thanks to their antioxidant power. There are 200 kinds of antioxidants found in nature, and just one mangosteen contains 40 of them. It is the most potent edible source of antioxidants in the world.
Mango	Mangoes contain high concentrations of vitamins A and C, and are also a good source of potassium and copper. This fruit restores health and detoxifies the liver. Its antioxidant properties are well-known.

Fruit	Health Benefits
Melon	As with all orange-fleshed foods, the melon provides provitamin A (carotene), and is rich in vitamins C and B, as well as in minerals, potassium in particular, and in various other dietary minerals (iron, zinc, copper, manganese, and iodine). Its fiber stimulates the bowels and has a slightly laxative effect, whereas its potassium content gives it diuretic properties. This fruit is recommended for people who suffer from constipation, hemorrhoids, rheumatism, arthritis, and pulmonary problems. Melon, a naturally low-calorie food, also helps the body eliminate toxins.
Blackberry	Blackberries are a great source of vitamin C and potassium, and contain magnesium and copper. This fortifying fruit is astringent, tonic, and very nutritious, acts as a purgative, a laxative, and anantihaemmorrhagic.
Orange	Best known for its wealth of vitamin C, the orange is often recommended as a natural blood thinner in cases of hypertension, anorexia, and shortness of breath. Low in calories, it contains fiber, water, "good carbohydrates," calcium, potassium, magnesium, and phosphorus. This citrus fruit is renowned for helping to reinforce the body's natural defenses against respiratory ailments, the flu, and other similar viruses by stimulating the immune system.
Grapefruit[1]	The grapefruit is rich in vitamin C and is a good source of potassium. It is also diuretic and tonic, helps promote liver drainage, protects capillaries and weak blood vessels, stimulates the appetite and digestion, and strengthens the stomach.
Papaya	Papaya is an excellent source of vitamin C and is a good source of vitamin A. Its precious enzyme (papain) promotes protein digestion and is known to have diuretic and stomachic properties. Papaya seeds are used to help the body expel intestinal parasites, and act as a powerful antioxidant agent used to help the body fight free radicals.
Peach	Peaches are very rich in fiber, hydrate the body, and contain potassium, calcium, vitamin C, and magnesium. Just one peach provides a good part of our daily-recommended intake of vitamin C, carotene, and fiber. Peaches also help ward off depression, and because they are low in calories, are an excellent addition to any weight loss program. The small red filaments in peach flesh, found close to the pit, contain flavonoid pigments, which strengthen the blood vessels, reducing the risks of varicose veins and rosacea.
Pear	Pears contain phosphorous, magnesium, carbohydrates, and a small amount of vitamin C. This nutritious fruit remineralizes, balances the body's pH, and helps prevent osteoporosis. Like its relative the apple, the pear is quite juicy, and hydrates and provides a good source of fiber, promoting healthy intestinal transit.

[1] A study published in the United States by Canadian researchers shows that grapefruit, orange, and apple juice could inhibit the absorption of certain medications and therefore greatly lower their efficiency. These are medications used to treat severe illnesses such as certain types of cancer, cardiovascular diseases, and infections, or to prevent the rejection of a transplanted organ.

Fruit	Health Benefits
Apple	Apples are primarily composed of water, fiber, potassium, calcium, carbohydrates, magnesium, and vitamin C. Eating the skin of the apple, which is richer in vitamin C than the flesh, is often recommended, but it must be thoroughly washed beforehand. This fruit has many health-giving virtues: it provides energy, lowers cholesterol, and helps eliminate kidney stones and prevent heart attacks. Thanks to their high fiber and water content, apples provide a feeling of fullness, making this fruit the perfect snack for people looking to maintain a healthy weight. Apples are also very rich in pectin, which limits and delays the absorption of sugar by the blood, helping to stave off hunger.
Plum	Plums contain vitamin C, magnesium, and calcium, as well as high levels of potassium and vitamins B and E, all of which help maintain the health of the heart, skin, intestines, and cells. This fruit is recommended in cases of hepatobiliary fatigue, constipation, and food poisoning, and contains a large amount of fiber, water, and sorbitol, which, together, make an effective laxative.
Grape	This fruit contains carbohydrates, water, fiber, phosphorous, potassium, vitamin C, and calcium. Rich in pigments and tannins, grapes have been shown to be beneficial to the small blood vessels that protect many of the linings in the body. Grapes are also a heart-healthy food thanks to their high concentration of polyphenols, protective pigments that help keep the cardiovascular system in good shape. However, due to their high sugar content, grapes are quite high in calories.

Fruits provide antioxidant activity that can play an important role in preventing cancers and other chronic illnesses. Eating more fruit is a logical step if you are trying to increase your antioxidant intake and reduce oxidative stress, which will ultimately lower your risk of cancer.

The highest levels of antioxidants can be found in berries: wild blueberries, blackberries, strawberries, raspberries, cranberries, and pomegranates.

After berries, the fruits richest in antioxidants are: plums, cherries, mangoes, apples, red grapes, kiwis, pineapples, oranges, lemons, grapefruits, peaches, pears, nectarines, and winter melons.

Numerous epidemiological studies have proven that diets rich in fruits and vegetables are associated with a lowered risk of cancer, metabolic syndrome, and osteoporosis. Most people are aware of the link between fruits, vegetables, and health, but still find it difficult to meet the daily-recommended intake of five servings of fruits and vegetables.

Fruits that are exceptionally high in fiber and antioxidants (including carotenoids, flavonoids, polyphenols, or vitamins C and E) are often called "superfruits," and berries and several types of exotic fruits are included in this group.

Smoothie Liquids

The fruits, vegetables, liquids, sugars, nutritional supplements, and recipes in this book are all suggestions to help you create your own delicious smoothies. Use your imagination to invent combinations according to your personal taste, your inspiration of the moment, and the products available to you.

Buttermilk

Buttermilk is an excellent source of potassium, vitamin B12, calcium, and riboflavin, and a good source of phosphorous. It contains zinc, magnesium, pantothenic acid, niacin, thiamine, folic acid, and vitamin B6. Rich in lactic acid and in nitrogen, buttermilk is low in fat, and suitable for people who suffer from digestive problems and high cholesterol.

Fresh cream

Whipping cream (35% milk fat) contains vitamin A. Cream provides energy because it is quite high in fat. However, its fats are composed of 62% saturated fatty acids, and because it is an animal fat, it is quite high in cholesterol. Depending on its fat content, cream contains from 10 to 38 mg of cholesterol/30 ml; it is an excellent food for people who are trying to gain weight, and to help combat dry skin.

Kefir

Dubbed "the centenary's beverage," kefir helps lower the risk of colon cancer. It is used as a healing food to treat various illnesses, mainly those of the digestive system such as gastroenteritis and stomach ulcers, and in the treatment of bronchitis and pneumonia. Kefir also has proven antitumor and antifungal properties.

Almond milk

Almond milk is an excellent source of calcium, magnesium, potassium, phosphorous, and essential fatty acids. Rich in fiber and protein and gluten free, this milk is one of the best sources of the antioxidant vitamin E, helping to slow down cellular and cutaneous aging.

Oat milk

Rich in calcium, potassium, magnesium, phosphorous, and in vitamins B1, B2, B3, D, E and K, oat milk is lactose and cholesterol free. It contains beta-glucans that reduce bad cholesterol and help with bowel movements. High in fiber, it is also rich in phytochemical compounds that help fight certain diseases such as cancer, and some heart diseases.

Goat's milk	Generally easy to digest, goat's milk is recommended for people who are allergic to the protein in cow's milk. It has many nutritional assets, thanks to its high iodine, phosphorous, and magnesium content.
Rice milk	Rice milk has a starchy flavor and no impact on blood sugar levels. Rich in slow sugars, it is generally prepared with whole grain rice syrup, rice starch, and water. Like oat milk, rice milk has a very neutral taste.
Soy milk	The low levels of saturated amino acids in this drink are very beneficial in regulating the level of cholesterol in the body. Soy milk contains lignans of phytoestrogens, and studies have shown a link between elevated lignan levels and a lowered risk of prostate, ovarian, and breast cancers, of osteoporosis, and of cardiovascular diseases.
Cow's milk	This milk contains very important proteins (each containing essential amino acids), high levels of calcium and vitamin D (prevents rickets), and is rich in riboflavin (B complex vitamins), vitamin A, magnesium, and fatty acids, namely omega-3 and omega-6.
Green tea	Green tea yields powerful antioxidant properties thanks to its polyphenols and flavonoids, which help effectively fight against free radicals, the elements chiefly responsible for aging, various cardiovascular diseases, and cancer.
Yogurt	An excellent source of protein, calcium, phosphorous, potassium, and vitamins A and B. Plain, unsweetened yogurt's nutritional value is very close to that of the milk used to prepare it, with the added benefits of fermentation. Fermentation benefits the digestive system, restoring, for example, the intestinal flora after an antibiotic treatment. It also helps prevent cancer and, when eaten before bed, encourages sleep.
Fruit or vegetable juice	For those who do not wish to use dairy, there is nothing like fruit and vegetable juices, which provide additional vitamins, possess excellent antioxidant properties, and give smoothies a nice texture and great flavor.
Water	Use tap, filtered, or bottled water, added as desired.

Green Smoothies

A green smoothie is a combination of fruits and leafy green vegetables, a delicious way to make sure you eat a large quantity of greens on a daily basis. Fruits cut the bitterness of certain green vegetables, making green smoothies an adult- and kid-friendly treat. Leafy greens provide chlorophyll, vitamins, minerals, an abundance of fiber, complete proteins and many, many illness-fighting phytonutrients that also improve our vitality and our overall health.

The following fruits taste delicious in green smoothies:

The banana, a classic, softens the taste of green vegetables while providing a creamy texture. Frozen fruits are particularly practical in the winter, but can be eaten year-round. Be adventurous and add vegetable-fruits such as the cucumber, tomato, avocado, and bell pepper.

The leaf stalks of root vegetables like carrots, beets, parsnips, radishes, and turnips, are excellent smoothie ingredients. You can also add in smaller quantities of sprouts, fine herbs such as basil, dill or mint, or even spicier-tasting greens such as arugula, mustard leaves, and watercress. Your taste and imagination are your only limits!

Vegetables

Vegetable	Health Benefits
Asparagus	Asparagus is renowned for its purgative, diuretic, laxative, and tonic virtues. Excellent for the waistline, it contains dietary minerals (magnesium, iron, manganese, copper and zinc), is rich in fiber, and also contains vitamins A (as much as in a tomato), B, C, and E, which helps slow cellular aging. Asparagus also contains glutathione, a substance possessing anticancer and antioxidant properties.
Avocado	The avocado is rich in vitamins E and B complex, and also contains potassium, magnesium, and amino acids. It is very rich in fats, which make it high in calories but also, thanks to its monounsaturated fatty acids, beneficial for the cardiovascular system and against hypertension.
Basil	Basil is packed with healing vitamin C and antioxidant vitamin A, and supplies calcium and phosphorous, both essential minerals in the proper development of bone tissue. This herb also clears up the respiratory passageways and is antiseptic.
Swiss chard	Raw, it is an excellent source of vitamins C and A, magnesium, and potassium. It also contains iron, copper, folate, riboflavin, vitamin B6, and calcium. Cooked, it is still an excellent source of potassium, magnesium, and vitamin A. It is also a source of vitamin C, iron, copper, riboflavin, and calcium. Chard leaves are known to be laxative and diuretic, and could also help reduce the risk of age-related vision loss, thanks to their lutein content.
Red beet	Beets are unique in in that they contain extremely high levels of carotenoids. Rich in carbohydrates and low in fat, they are an excellent source of folate and full of antioxidants that help the body fight against heart disease and certain cancers, particularly of the colon. Its leaves are also rich in beta-carotene, folate, chlorophyll, potassium, vitamin C, and iron.
Broccoli	Exceptionally rich in vitamins, broccoli has one of the highest levels of vitamin C out of all of the green vegetables. It supplies antioxidant provitamin A and vitamin B9, which helps reduce the risk of colon cancer. It is high in fiber, great for the bowels, and high in sulfurous elements, which are also present in cabbage, known to be beneficial in preventing cancer. The water found in broccoli is high in minerals: potassium, calcium, phosphorous, and magnesium. It helps reduce the risk of developing certain cancers (breast, colon, and stomach) because it is rich in beta-carotene, fiber, and in phytochemical compounds.
Carrot	The carrot is the greatest plant source of provitamin A. Its antioxidant compounds help protect against cardiovascular diseases and cancer, while also promoting better vision.
Celery	Celery provides calcium, iron, potassium, sodium, vitamins A, B and C, and is rich in potassium. Because it has diuretic properties, it is an effective food in fighting against hypertension as well as rheumatic issues, gout, and renal colic.

Vegetable	Health Benefits
Kale	Loaded with vitamin C, kale is also a good source of vitamin E as well as pro-vitamin A, both precious antioxidants that protect against harmful environmental elements. It is also rich in minerals, mainly potassium, and studies have shown it to be an excellent anticancer food. Kale is a veritable arsenal of vitamins that contains so many beneficial substances (sulfur, most notably) that eating it just twice a week would significantly reduce the risk of cancer, lung cancer in particular.
Cucumber	The cucumber contains an abundance of dietary minerals, most notably potassium, phosphorous, and calcium. Consequently, it is a very effective purgative and diuretic. This crunchy vegetable is a source of most vitamins, particularly many of the B complex vitamins. Its skin contains provitamin A and vitamin E, which helps stave off cellular aging. High in fiber, it promotes bowel health and is easy to digest thanks to the pepsin it contains.
Squash	The pumpkin contains carotenoids that help the body fight cancer, most notably of the colon and breast, and diabetes. The vitamins in the pumpkin also help protect against cardiovascular diseases. The brightly colored varieties of squash are rich in provitamin A, or carotene. Winter squash, for example, owes its bright orange-yellow color to this element; the pigment is made up of over 80% of the antioxidant carotene, which helps reduce cellular alterations in the body. All squash is rich in fiber.
Zucchini	Composed of nearly 95% water, the zucchini contains dietary minerals, potassium, phosphorous, magnesium, calcium, vitamin B3, and provitamin A. It is a source of fiber, which promotes bowel health; it also contains pectin and lutein, which helps maintain eye health. A potassium-rich diet is known to reduce hypertension, making this vegetable a good shield for the cardiovascular system.
Watercress	Containing high levels of vitamins, starting with vitamin C, watercress also fulfills the daily requirement of provitamin A, a precious antioxidant, which fights the dangerous effects of free radicals. A leader among fresh vegetables in calcium content, it also contributes to preventing hypertension, much like magnesium. Studies have revealed watercress' protective action against cardiovascular diseases thanks to the polyunsaturated fatty acids it contains, as well as against the development of certain cancers thanks to its cancer-fighting sulfurous substances.
Spinach	Spinach's green leaves are positively bursting with minerals. Among the leafy greens, it ranks impressively high in potassium, calcium, and magnesium content. It also supplies iron and large quantities of vitamins—vitamin C, folate, and carotene (provitamin A). These substances are powerful antioxidants that protect the body against the premature aging of cells and the development of certain cancers. Moreover, on top of pigments (chlorophyll and carotene), spinach contains flavonoids; these substances act together to reinforce vitamin C's properties, and to protect the capillaries.

Vegetable	Health Benefits
Ginger	Ginger can lower blood pressure and increase circulation thanks to its compound gingerol. It helps relieve motion sickness, morning sickness, and pain-induced nausea. Additionally, its antioxidant compounds help prevent cardiovascular diseases as well as certain cancers.
Lettuce	Containing a tremendous amount of water, lettuce has very few calories, most leafy vegetables. Lettuce provides the body with a wide variety of dietary minerals, most notably potassium, calcium, phosphorous, and magnesium. Its vitamin C content is impressive, and is concentrated in its darker leaves; this green also provides vitamin B, provitamin A, and vitamin E. Thanks to its vitamins, it is particularly effective in limiting cellular aging and lowering the risk of cardiovascular diseases. Lettuce also provides dietary fiber, essential in the fight against cardiovascular and gastrointestinal issues.
Green mint	Long known for its calming, analgesic, and anesthetic virtues, mint not only soothes pain, but also can be used as a respiratory and digestive antiseptic. It is also quite beneficial to the digestive system as an effective appetite stimulant.
Parsley	Parsley is very rich in antioxidant vitamin C and carotene (provitamin A). Curly or flat-leafed, it is also high in dietary minerals. Even though it is typically only eaten it in small quantities, it provides potassium, calcium, magnesium, and iron. Quite useful in helping fight against anemia, it is also known for its virtues as a tonic. It also has sedative properties, and gives a feeling of calm and serenity.
Bell pepper	The bell pepper's high fiber content stimulates the bowels, and its vitamin C content, just slightly lower than parsley's, is even higher than that of cabbage and spinach. A bell pepper is an excellent source of carotene (provitamin A) and flavonoids (vitamin P), present in its pigments. The former provide excellent antioxidant properties and prevent both the premature aging of cells and tumor formation. The latter reinforce the benefits of vitamin C and offer some protection to small blood vessels (the riper and redder the pepper, the more of these precious pigments it contains).
Tomato	The tomato is an excellent source of vitamin C as well as carotene and vitamin E, whose antioxidant virtues stimulate the body's natural defenses. Studies have proven its preventative action against the development of certain cancers, namely of the prostate and the lungs, thanks to its high lycopene content, which endows it with its red hue. The tomato is also very rich in dietary minerals, notably in potassium, which plays a role in regulating kidney activity. Its phosphorous, calcium, and magnesium contents are also quite high. The tomato's skin and seeds contain fibers that stimulate the bowels.

Nutritional Supplements

It is up to you to decide whether or not to add a nutritional supplement to your smoothie. Obviously, some supplements have a neutral taste, whereas others will have a stronger flavor. Personalize your smoothie according to your preferences, tastes, and nutritional needs.

Cocoa

This basic ingredient in chocolate is rich in magnesium and provides iron, phosphorous, calcium, and potassium. It also contains tonic substances, mainly theobromine, caffeine, phenylethylamine, and serotonin. It is an important source of dietary minerals, contains fiber, and is a balanced source of vitamins.

Carob

Carob powder can be taken as a dietary supplement to help deal with various health issues. Its grains contain less fat compared with cocoa's. Carob contains more fiber and calcium, with a sugar and saccharose content of 40%, 35% starch, and 7% protein. Carob grains contain iron, calcium, phosphorous, and magnesium.

Spices
(ginger, clove, vanilla, cinnamon)

Herbs and spices have concentrated antioxidants, with levels that surpass those of many plants. They help limit the oxidative stress that is involved in the aging of cells. Use them in moderation to avoid overpowering the flavor of the fruits and vegetables!

Fresh fine herbs
(basil, parsley, mint, thyme, sage, chives, etc.)

Basil, cilantro, mint, and other fresh herbs will enhance your blend, and will also add their fair share of antioxidants. Their high flavonoid content endows them with cancer-fighting properties. Depending on the herb, they have varying strengths of antifungal, antiviral, and antibacterial properties.

Royal jelly

A superfood with exceptional vitalizing and energizing properties, royal jelly has no equal; it is prescribed to treat asthma, chronic fatigue, and depression, and helps speed up the healing process.

Wheat germ

Wheat germ is a natural source of vitamin B and vitamin E, minerals (phosphorous, magnesium, and iron) and the dietary mineral zinc. It also plays an important role in protecting skin cells against free radicals.

Ginkgo biloba

Both a tonic and a vascular protector, ginkgo biloba has vasodilating and antioxidant effects, which are linked to limiting the accumulation of blood platelets. These properties increase the blood supply to the brain, helping to prevent strokes. It is also considered to be as effective as many prescription drugs in the treatment of various cognitive ailments. Most notably, it slows the onset of Alzheimer's, improves the cognitive faculties, and is a popular supplement in the treatment of senile dementia.

Ginseng

Ginseng contains numerous vitamins—B1, B2, and B3—and minerals such as iron, aluminum, copper and sulfur. It helps the body cope with stress, yet acts simultaneously as a stimulant without the negative side effects of synthetic stimulants. Ginseng strengthens the immune system, rebalances and regenerates various bodily functions, increases stress resistance, and improves blood circulation. It also improves physical and intellectual performance: it strengthens the memory and concentration, improves reflexes, allows the body to better adapt to hard physical work, reduces the feeling of fatigue as well as muscle pain, slows the effects of aging, and rehydrates dry skin.

Flaxseeds

These seeds are extremely good for the health thanks to their essential fatty acids as well as their lignan content, phenolic compounds that share common characteristics with certain sex hormones, which work together with the body's estrogen receptors. They are considered phytoestrogens.

Lecithin

Lecithin contains essential fatty acids, certain B complex vitamins, and precious phospholipids. It helps move the fat found in the blood and limits fatty deposits in the arteries. Lecithin is also vital to brain cells and nerves, is a natural calming agent, and improves concentration; lecithin taken daily over the course of six months has been shown to improve the memory of people suffering from Alzheimer's disease. Those with high cholesterol, high blood pressure, cardiovascular issues, or clogged arteries should consider taking lecithin supplements; it is very beneficial for nerve cells and the proper metabolism of fat.

Brewer's yeast

Yeast is a treasure trove of nutritional substances: it contains proteins, lecithin, the most essential amino acids, a powerful detoxifier and antioxidant, glutathione, mineral salts, and dietary minerals, vitamins—including the entire B complex series—, and provitamin D. Because it is fortifying, it helps fight fatigue, and it is also said to help delay premature aging and increase intellectual performance.

Omega-3 and omega-6

These fatty acids help reduce triglyceride levels in the blood, a risk factor for cardiovascular diseases. They also improve blood flow and help reduce plaque deposits, which can lead to heart attacks or strokes. Omega-3 and omega-6 can be found in dark green, leafy vegetables and wild herbs such as lamb's lettuce, purslane, spinach, and watercress. They are also present in the oil and seeds of hemp and flax, as well as in canola oil, which contains an ideal balance of omega-3 and omega-6.

Pollen	Pollen is very rich in B complex vitamins, most notably in vitamin B5, which is recommended for hair loss prevention. It is also rich in vitamins A, E, and C, and in minerals such as iron, magnesium, and phosphorous. Its protein content and, more specifically, its essential amino and sulfuric acid content makes it an ideal supplement for cases of fatigue linked to a nutritional imbalance. One of nature's better remineralizing agents, it is also an effective antioxidant against free radicals.
Probiotics	Probiotics are healthy bacteria that lend a hand in strengthening the immune system by way of the intestines. Available in capsules and present in kefir, yogurt, and fermented milk, they help balance the intestinal flora, improve the colon's microflora, and improve overall digestion. Probiotics also improve lactose tolerance, help with vitamin absorption, stimulate the immune system, and promote bowel health.
Spirulina	Spirulina is packed with vitamins, dietary minerals, mineral salts, carbohydrates, fatty acids, and plant proteins. A therapeutic anti-fatigue food, it is useful against demineralization, and is energizing, a nervous tonic, and gives a boost to people who require elevated energy levels, such as athletes and the overworked.

Sweeteners

Sweetening your smoothie is not always necessary, given that fruits have many naturally occurring sugars.

Honey	Honey adds more sweetness than sugar, but also has a more pronounced, distinguishable flavor.
Agave syrup	This neutral-tasting syrup is extracted from the sap at the heart of the agave plant. It is very sweet and high in fructose.
Maple syrup	Use maple syrup sparingly, as it has a very distinct taste. It is an excellent antioxidant.
Cane syrup	Mostly used in Caribbean cuisine, cane syrup is has a potent sweetness and a neutral taste.
Stevia	Stevia's sweetening strength is 10 to 15 times higher than sugar's. It is used to lower blood pressure and blood sugar levels.

The Tools

The Blender

The standard blender has a base that houses the motor, blades that turn and chop the food, and a container. It can mix large quantities of food and beverages, and its motor is powerful enough to mix all kinds of ingredients, even crushed ice, although some blenders are much more powerful than others. When selecting a model, choose one with removable blades so that you can easily clean them. If you want to be able to crush ice for your smoothies, choose a blender with a container that is made out of glass rather than plastic. In any case, the unit should be solid enough to blend frozen fruits and to crush ice.

The hand blender could be an interesting and space-saving choice. However, it does not crush ice.

The Juicer

A juicer is useful if you wish to make your own fruit and vegetable juices. Learn about the different models and available features before choosing your home juicer. Does it extract the juice of any vegetable? Does the machine tend to oxidize the juice more quickly? Is the opening large enough to insert all sizes of fruits and vegetables?

Various Utensils

Measuring spoons and cups, for the precise measuring of liquids and solids

A silicone spatula to empty the blender without damaging it

A cutting board

A cherry pitter, or one for any other type of stone fruit

An apple corer

Sharp knives

A zester

A citrus press

Straws for decoration

Glasses

Serve your smoothies in a variety of different glasses.

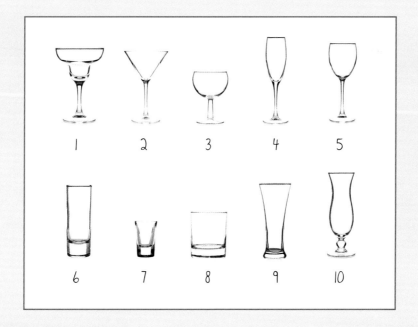

1	Margarita glass (270 ml)	
2	Martini or cocktail glass (70 to 120 ml)	
3	Champagne coupe (160 ml)	
4	Champagne flute (160 ml)	
5	Wine glass (balloon) (150 to 250 ml)	

1 Margarita glass (270 ml)

2 Martini or cocktail glass (70 to 120 ml)

3 Champagne coupe (160 ml)

4 Champagne flute (160 ml)

5 Wine glass (balloon) (150 to 250 ml)

6 Highball glass (240 to 350 ml)

7 Shooter glass (liqueur glass) (50 to 100 ml)

8 Whisky tumbler (old-fashioned) (150 to 330 ml)

9 Beer glass (250 ml)

10 Tulip glass (150 ml)

Smoothies for a Healthy Heart

There is a direct link between a healthy diet and a lowered risk of arterial hypertension and heart disease; maintaining healthy eating habits reduces cholesterol, sodium, and saturated and trans fats.

Avocado and Green Apple

Avocado and Green Apple

1/2 cup (125 ml) water
1 green apple
1/2 ripe avocado
1 tbsp lime juice

In a blender, or with a hand blender, purée all ingredients until smooth. Drink immediately.

Avocados are an excellent source of antioxidants. They also help protect the heart and prevent strokes.

Protein Punch!

3 servings

1-1/2 cups (375 ml) skim milk
1/2 cup (125 ml) mango juice
1/2 cup (125 ml) blueberries
1/2 cup (125 ml) strawberries
1/4 cup (60 ml) sliced or ground almonds
1 tbsp ground flaxseeds
1 tbsp real maple syrup
1 tsp fresh ginger, grated

In a blender, purée all ingredients for 1 minute, until smooth. Serve in large, chilled glasses.

Try this smoothie with almond or rice milk! People who practice endurance sports prize the almonds and flaxseeds in this powerful smoothie for the protein and unsaturated fats they provide, and the blueberries for their high concentration of quercetin, which encourages cellular oxygenation.

Cardio Cocktail

Cardio Cocktail

2 peaches or nectarines, unpeeled, pitted and cut into pieces, or
1/2 cup (125 ml) berries
1/4 cup (60 ml) plain yogurt (Balkan-style)
1 tbsp honey
4 fresh mint leaves
Crushed ice

In a blender, purée all ingredients until smooth. Drink immediately.

Use any combination of strawberries, blackberries, blueberries, raspberries, or blackcurrants. The polyphenols found in berries contribute to cardiovascular health and improve the elasticity of blood vessel walls.

Perfect Pear and Apple

2 servings

2 apples, cored and cut into pieces
2 pears, cored and cut into pieces
1 cup (250 ml) orange juice, freshly pressed
1 cup (250 ml) yogurt
1 tsp honey
Crushed ice

In a blender, purée all ingredients until smooth. Serve.

Both apples and pears are rich in fiber and antioxidants, and reduce cholesterol and fat absorption in the intestines. The high concentration of antioxidants in pear skin helps prevent cardiovascular disease and certain types of cancer.

Guava, Mango and Coconut Trio

2 guavas, peeled and quartered
1 very ripe mango, diced
1/4 cup (60 ml) coconut milk
1 pinch nutmeg
Juice and zest of **1** lime
Crushed ice

Thin out guava pulp with a bit of ice water. Press pulp through a wire mesh strainer to collect the juice (approximately 1/2 cup (125 ml), depending on the size of the guava).

In a blender, combine guava juice and diced mango. Add coconut milk, nutmeg, lime juice, and zest, and purée until smooth. Serve with crushed ice.

Guava helps lower cholesterol levels as well as arterial tension. This exotic cocktail protects the heart thanks to its high concentration of antioxidants.

Smoothies for Arthritis

Some of the most common problems among arthritis sufferers are the unwanted side effects of certain medications used to treat this condition, which can include fatigue, digestive trouble, nausea, dizziness, and depression. Making a few simple dietary changes can help alleviate these negative side effects, improving the quality of life of many arthritis patients.

Banana Mangosteen

2 servings

1/2 banana
1 cup (250 ml) mangosteen, peeled and cut into pieces
1 cup (250 ml) pineapple juice
1 tbsp real maple syrup
1 tbsp propolis

In a blender, or with a hand blender, purée all ingredients until smooth. Serve.

The mangosteen is a round, purplish fruit, about the size of a golf ball. Its rind, or exocarp, is thick, bitter, and inedible, and its sweet, slightly acidic white flesh is divided into four to eight segments.

Pineapples contain bromelain, while bananas are alkalizing and the mangosteen has antioxidant properties. The perfect cocktail to help soothe joint pain caused by arthritis!

Propolis is sold raw, as a concentrated extract, or as a mother tincture, and can be purchased from authorized beekeepers.

Flex Cocktail

Flex Cocktail

1 apple, cored and cut into pieces
1 celery stalk, cut into pieces
2 cucumbers, cut into rounds

There are two ways to prepare this smoothie:
1. Juice all ingredients in a juicer. Serve.
2. In a blender, or with a hand blender, purée all ingredients until smooth. Add a bit of water, strain with a wire mesh strainer, and serve.

In Ayurvedic medicine (a form of traditional South Asian medicine), celery is used to treat rheumatoid arthritis and gout, while cucumber is used for its powerful cleansing properties to eliminate toxins, including uric acid, helping to relieve arthritis pain.

Magnificent Melon

2 servings

1/2 cantaloupe, cut into pieces
1 cup (250 ml) almond milk
2 tsp honey or agave syrup

In a blender, or with a hand blender, purée all ingredients until smooth. Serve.

Try adding cantaloupe and almond milk to your diet to help manage pain caused by arthritis or arthrosis!

Spiru-Berry

Spiru-Berry

2 servings

1/4 cup (60 ml) water
1/4 cup (60 ml) strawberries or blueberries
1/2 banana
1/4 cup (60 ml) soy milk
1/2 cup (125 ml) plain yogurt
1 tbsp ground flaxseeds
1 tsp spirulina powder

In a blender, or with a hand blender, purée all ingredients until smooth. Serve.

Start your day with this delicious combination of antioxidant-rich berries, flaxseeds, and spirulina. A true breakfast of champions!

Giving Greens

1 serving

1/2 cup (125 ml) water
Juice of **1** lime
3 kiwis, peeled and sliced
1 cup (250 ml) mâche (also called lamb's lettuce or corn salad)
1 avocado, cut into pieces
1/2 banana
Crushed ice

In a blender, or with a hand blender, purée all ingredients, except crushed ice, until smooth. Garnish with a slice of kiwi and serve with crushed ice.

Instead of mâche, try spinach, arugula, or watercress!

This recipe is a favorite of raw foodies: it is packed with vitamins and tastes slightly spicy and pleasantly tart.

Avocado helps combat arthritis pain. Bananas and kiwis contain health-giving antioxidants and are recommended to help boost the immune system.

43

Smoothies to Improve the Memory

Studies have proven that fruits that are high in antioxidants, polyphenols, and vitamin C help prevent the onset of Alzheimer's disease.

Brainy Beet

1 large beet, peeled and cut into pieces
1 orange, cut into pieces
1 tsp fresh ginger, chopped
1/2 cup (125 ml) grapefruit juice
1 tbsp agave syrup

In a blender, or with a hand blender, purée all ingredients until smooth. Serve.

Drinking beet juice every day increases blood flow to the brain and improves memory. Because of its high nitrate content, beet juice also helps prevent dementia. Oranges and grapefruit are an excellent source of vitamin C.

Very Strawberry

Very Strawberry

2 servings

15 small strawberries
10 blueberries
10 green or red grapes
1/2 banana
1/2 cup (125 ml) plain yogurt

In a blender, or with a hand blender, purée all ingredients until smooth. Serve.

Stock up on polyphenols with strawberries, blueberries, and grapes!

Strawberry Blackcurrant

4 servings

1 cup (250 ml) strawberries
1/2 cup (125 ml) blackcurrants
1/2 cup (125 ml) plain yogurt
1 tbsp honey
1 tsp lavender flowers (optional)
Crushed ice

In a blender, purée all ingredients until smooth. Strain and serve.

Blackcurrants are one of the best natural fruit sources of vitamin C. Strawberries and blackcurrants have powerful antioxidant properties!

Grape and Blueberry

2 servings

1-1/2 cups (375 ml) grape juice
1-1/2 cups (375 ml) blueberries
1/2 cup (125 ml) plain yogurt
1/2 banana

In a blender, or with a hand blender, purée all ingredients until smooth. Serve.

Studies have shown that the natural pigments in blueberries and grapes help improve memory.

Green Tea and Pineapple

2 servings

1/4 cup (60 ml) green tea, infused
1/4 cup (60 ml) coconut milk or plain yogurt
1 tsp lemon juice
1/4 cup (60 ml) fresh pineapple, peeled
and cubed
1 mango, cut into pieces
1 tsp fresh ginger, grated
Crushed ice

In a blender, purée all ingredients
for 30 to 60 seconds until smooth. Serve.

Theanine is a unique amino acid found in green tea that increases seratonin and dopamine levels in the brain. Pineapple and mango are rich in vitamin C, and ginger is a powerful antioxidant.

Smoothies for Diabetes

A controlled, carefully monitored diet is an essential part of diabetes treatment, along with regular physical activity and medication.

Zesty Avocado

1-1/2 avocados, cut into pieces
1 tbsp orange zest
1 tsp fresh ginger, grated
1 tsp salt
1 pinch black pepper
2 cups (500 ml) milk

GARNISH
1/2 avocado, sliced
1 tbsp lemon juice

In a blender, or with a hand blender, purée all ingredients until smooth. Garnish with avocado slices sprinkled with lemon juice. Serve.

Avocado is creamy, rich, and loaded with health-giving unsaturated fat. It also slows digestion and helps prevent a spike in blood sugar after a meal.

Watermelon Banana

1/2 cup (125 ml) water
2 cups (500 ml) watermelon, seeded and cut into pieces
1 banana, cut into pieces
2 cups (500 ml) baby spinach
Crushed ice (optional)

In a blender, or with a hand blender, purée ingredients until smooth, except baby spinach. Add spinach and pulse until smooth. Serve with crushed ice, if desired.

Watermelon contains citrulline and arginine. Citrulline improves the health of the heart and the immune system, helps control diabetes, and stimulates weight loss. Arginine is a powerful detoxifying agent and helps treat erectile dysfunction.

Zesty Avocado

Sweet Swiss Chard

2 servings

1 cup (250 ml) water
1/2 banana
1/2 papaya, peeled and seeded
2 Swiss chard leaves

In a blender, or with a hand blender, purée all ingredients until smooth. Serve.

Red Swiss chard contains many antioxidants. It is also used in traditional Turkish medicine to help fight diabetes. Papaya also helps prevent and treat diabetes.

Get Your Greens

4 servings

1 cup (250 ml) water
1 cup (250 ml) mâche (also called lamb's lettuce or corn salad) or Boston lettuce
2 cups (500 ml) baby spinach
3 ripe pears
1 pinch cinnamon

In a blender, or with a hand blender, purée all ingredients until smooth. Serve.

The antioxidants in green vegetables prevent type 2 diabetes by fighting against free radicals.

Kiwi Avocado

1 cup (250 ml) white grape juice
1 kiwi, peeled and cut into pieces
1/2 avocado, cut into pieces
1 pinch fresh ginger, grated
2 tbsp ground flaxseed

Spread kiwi pieces on a baking sheet
and freeze for 1 hour.

In a blender, or with a hand blender,
purée all ingredients until smooth. Serve.

Kiwis are packed with fiber, and a diet rich in fiber helps prevent cardiovascular diseases, control type 2 diabetes, and regulate the appetite.

The Big Blue

2 **cups (500 ml)** milk
1-1/2 cups (375 ml) berries of your choice
1/2 cup (125 ml) plain yogurt
1 tbsp maple syrup

In a blender, or with a hand blender, purée ingredients until smooth. Serve.

Red and blue berries contain anthocyanins, naturally-occurring compounds that scientific research suggests may contribute to lowering blood sugar by stimulating insulin production.

The Baby Blue

2 servings

1/2 cup (125 ml) blueberries
1 cup (250 ml) soy milk
2 tbsp ground chia seeds or flaxseeds
1 tsp stevia

In a blender, or with a hand blender, purée all ingredients until smooth. Serve.

Blueberries stimulate insulin production by regenerating pancreatic cells, while chia seeds are naturally rich in dietary fiber and healthy fat (omega-3). Chia provides 100% of the recommended daily intake of omega-3.

The Big Blue

Smoothies for Intestinal Transit

For a healthy intestinal transit time (the time it takes for food to move through the entire digestive tract), the body needs 30g of fiber per day. To improve intestinal transit, eat a piece of fresh fruit in the morning, fresh-cut vegetables with meals, and another piece of fresh fruit for dessert. Drinking at least six cups of magnesium-rich water is also strongly recommended. Milk and fermented dairy products also help balance intestinal flora.

Strawberry Banana

Strawberry Banana

2 cups (500 ml) strawberries, cut into pieces
2 tbsp real maple syrup
2 tbsp lemon juice
2 bananas, cut into pieces
1-1/2 cups (375 ml) plain yogurt
A few fresh mint leave

In a bowl, combine strawberries, maple syrup, and lemon juice. Let sit for a few minutes to allow the strawberries to release their juices.

In a blender, or with a hand blender, purée all ingredients until smooth. Serve.

Strawberries are loaded with vitamin C. In addition to being a good source of cellulose, this berry also acts as a diuretic, improves intestinal transit, and facilitates digestion. Bananas are high in fiber and promote normal bowel function.

Think Pink

2 servings

1/2 cup (125 ml) milk
1 cup (250 ml) raspberries
1/2 cup (125 ml) plain probiotic yogurt
1 tbsp stevia

In a blender, or with a hand blender, purée all ingredients until smooth. Serve.

Raspberries are effective in treating constipation, thanks to their high fiber content. Taken regularly, probiotics (lactobacillus) keep the intestines functioning optimally.

Strawberry Apple

3 servings

3/4 cup (180 ml) apple juice
10 strawberries
4 red apples, cored, peeled, and cut into pieces
Crushed ice
1 tbsp real maple syrup

In a blender, or with a hand blender, pulse together apple juice, strawberries, apples, and crushed ice, until smooth. Add maple syrup and continue puréeing until creamy. Serve.

Super Fresh Smoothie

2 servings

Juice of **1** orange
1 apple, cored, peeled, and cut into pieces
1 pear, cored, peeled, and cut into pieces
2 kiwis, peeled and cut into pieces

There are two ways to prepare this smoothie:
1. Juice the ingredients in a juicer. Serve.
2. In a blender, or with a hand blender, purée all ingredients until smooth. Serve.

Oranges are rich in vitamin C, and apples are high in fiber. Pears contain vitamins A and B, and have powerful antioxidant properties. Kiwis are an excellent source of vitamin C, fiber, and potassium. These all add up to make the perfect digestive aid smoothie!

Strawberry Apple

Plummy Fig Smoothie

2 servings

3/4 cup (180 ml) apple juice
2 plums, pitted
1/2 banana
2 dried figs
Crushed ice

In a blender, purée all ingredients until smooth. Serve.

Many types of fruit contain fiber, which helps prevent and relieve constipation, including: citrus fruits (oranges, grapefruits, pomelos), pears, apples (without the skin), plums, prunes, figs, dates, grapes, strawberries, blackberries, raspberries, guavas (without the skin), pineapples, mangoes, and bananas.

Smoothies for Healthy Bones

To fight osteoporosis, it is important to follow a diet low in protein as well as alcohol, coffee, and salt. It is highly recommended to eat at least four servings of calcium-rich dairy per day (including yogurt, cheese, milk, etc.) to strengthen the bones, as well as to get enough sun exposure (vitamin D helps absorb calcium), exercise regularly, eat three meals a day, and drink plenty of water.

Greens and Apple

1 serving

1/4 cup (60 ml) water
1 apple, cored and cut into pieces
2 sprigs parsley
1 cup (250 ml) spinach (or mâche)
1/2 banana

In a blender, or with a hand blender, purée all ingredients until smooth. If mixture is too thick, add a bit of water. Serve.

Substitute the water with almond, soy, or rice milk, or kefir. Add some spirulina to your smoothie!

Did you know that just 1/2 cup of spinach provides the recommended daily intake of vitamin K, which is essential to bone health? Vitamin K deficiency can lead to reduced bone density and an increased risk of fractures in post-menopausal women and women over 60.

Red Currant

1 cup (250 ml) 2% milk
1 cup (250 ml) red currants
1/2 banana
1 peach or pear, chopped
1 tbsp real maple syrup
Crushed ice

In a blender, purée all ingredients until smooth. Serve.

Use rice milk, soy milk, or almond milk! The red currant's biggest attribute is its high vitamin C content: it contains 40 mg of vitamin C, a level close to that of some citrus fruits, which have the advantage, thanks to their high concentration of certain flavonoid pigments.

Berry Good

1/2 cup (125 ml) almond milk
1 cup (250 ml) berries of your choice
2 tbsp honey

In a blender, or with a hand blender, purée all ingredients until smooth. Serve.

Strawberries, blackcurrants, cherries, blackberries, and blueberries, combined with almond milk, help prevent osteoporosis. Plus, blackcurrants are extremely rich in vitamins C and E, and are a powerful antioxidant.

Strawberry Kiwi

2 servings

1/4 cup (60 ml) light coconut milk
1 cup (250 ml) strawberries
1 kiwi, peeled and sliced
1 cup (250 ml) skim milk (or soy milk)
1 cup (250 ml) low-fat yogurt
1 tbsp honey

In a blender, or with a hand blender, purée all ingredients until smooth. Serve in chilled glasses.

Strawberries and kiwis are high in calcium and potassium. They also contain antioxidants, which help strengthen bones by helping to prevent bone demineralization. Paired with milk, these two fruits make one of the best anti-osteoporosis cocktails!

Calcium Boost

1/2 banana
1 cup (250 ml) raspberries
2 tbsp goji berries
1 orange, cut into pieces
2 tbsp sesame seeds
1/2 tbsp maca powder
1 tbsp agave syrup
1 cup (250 ml) water

In a blender, or using a hand blender, purée all ingredients until smooth. Serve.

This smoothie provides 47% of the recommended daily intake of calcium: sesame seeds provide 28%, and the rest comes from the orange (6%), the goji berries (6%), the raspberries (4%), the banana (1%), and the maca (2%), often called Peruvian ginseng, although it is not a member of the ginseng family.

Smoothies for Cholesterol

People who consume plenty of fruits and vegetables generally have low cholesterol. Fresh fruit contains vitamins, fiber, and antioxidants, which promote healthy cholesterol levels.

Polyphenol Cocktail

3 servings

1/2 cup (125 ml) green tea
1/2 cup (125 ml) pomegranate juice
2 cups (500 ml) berries of your choice
1/2 cup (125 ml) plain yogurt
1 tbsp organic dark cocoa powder

In a blender, or with a hand blender, purée all ingredients until smooth. If desired, thin out with a bit of green tea. Serve very cold.

To prepare green tea, infuse 1-1/2 tsp Kukicha tea leaves in 2/3 cup (160 ml) boiling water. Polyphenols are most effective when taken with meals, helping to prevent the oxidation of bad cholesterol, which, in turn, helps prevent clogged arteries. This smoothie is positively packed with polyphenols!

Apricantaloupe

6 fresh apricots, left unpeeled, pitted
1 cup (250 ml) cantaloupe, roughly chopped
1/2 cup (125 ml) plain yogurt

In a blender, or with a hand blender, purée all ingredients until smooth. Chill for 30 minutes before serving.

Load up on carotene by eating plenty of apricots and cantaloupe. These fruits also protect against different types of heart disease.

Strawberry Almond

4 servings

2 cups (500 ml) almond milk
2 cups (500 ml) strawberries
2 tbsp soft tofu
1 tbsp cane syrup
Crushed ice
A few fresh mint leaves

In a blender, purée all ingredients until smooth. Top with mint and serve.

Soft tofu, also known as silken tofu, should be stored in water and will keep in the refrigerator for 7 to 10 days. Change the tofu water daily. Oleaginous fruits, such as almonds, contain unsaturated fats that help lower bad cholesterol.

Pomegranate Punch

1 cup (250 ml) pomegranate juice
1/2 cup (125 ml) soy milk
1/2 banana
2 tbsp ground almonds
1 tsp agave syrup (or stevia)
Crushed ice

In a blender, purée all ingredients until smooth. Serve.

The antioxidant activity of pomegranates is higher than that of red wine and green tea, and their juice prevents the oxidation of bad cholesterol.

Lycopapaya

1/2 cup (125 ml) oat milk
1/2 cup (125 ml) fresh papaya
1/2 cup (125 ml) tomato juice
1 tbsp sugar
1 tsp vanilla
Crushed ice

In a blender, purée all ingredients until smooth. Serve.

The lycopene in papaya and tomatoes and the beta-glucans in oat milk help reduce bad cholesterol.

Smoothies to Fight Cancer

Rich in fiber, vitamins, minerals, nutrients, antioxidants, and phenolic compounds, smoothies are the quintessential anticancer food! Smoothies also eliminate toxins that have accumulated in the body due to a fat-heavy diet.

Pinapple Turmeric

1 fresh pineapple, peeled and roughly chopped
1/2 **cup (125 ml)** light coconut milk
1 **tbsp** turmeric
1/2 **tsp** black pepper

In a blender, or with a hand blender, purée all ingredients until smooth. Serve.

Coconut milk is produced by soaking shredded coconut meat in boiling water. It can be bought in cans or prepared at home. To prepare it at home, combine 1/2 cup shredded, unsweetened coconut with 1 cup hot water, milk, or coconut water in a pot and cover the mixture for 30 minutes. Then, drain the mixture and let sit. A layer of coconut cream will form on the surface, and this cream can be mixed with the milk, or removed. Coconut milk is three times higher in calories than whole milk and contains more saturated fat than both milk and cream.

Bromelain, the active ingredient in pineapple, inhibits the production of prostaglandins in the body that cause inflammation, thins the blood, and boosts the immune system. Combined with turmeric and pepper, bromelain makes an excellent tonic and digestive aid and, most importantly, it helps fight cancer!

Beet and Grapefruit

4 servings

1 medium red beet, cooked, peeled,
and roughly chopped
3/4 cup (180 ml) fresh grapefruit juice
Juice of **2** oranges, freshly pressed
1 tbsp fresh ginger, grated
1 tbsp cane syrup

In a blender, or with a hand blender, purée
all ingredients until smooth. Serve.

*The beet is an excellent cancer-fighting food. Citrus has been shown to
reduce the risk of cancer. Ginger activates the immune system.*

Blue Pomegranate

1 serving

1 cup (250 ml) pomegranate juice
1-1/2 cups (375 ml) blueberries
1 tbsp honey

In a blender, or with a hand blender, purée
all ingredients until smooth. If desired,
thin out the mixture by adding more
pomegranate juice. Serve.

Use cane sugar instead of honey!

*The antioxidant activity of pomegranates is higher than that of red wine,
or even green tea! The fruit, well known for its anti-inflammatory effects
and high level of antioxidants that protect the body against damage caused
by free radicals, also contains isoflavones, which are organic compounds
that play an important role in apoptosis, or programmed cell death.*

A.M. Turmeric

1 tsp turmeric
1 tbsp olive oil
1/2 cup (125 ml) tomato juice (or vegetable juice)
1 pinch black pepper

In a large glass, combine turmeric and olive oil, and stir until well blended. Add tomato juice and pepper and mix well. Serve.

Turmeric is one of nature's most powerful healers, and has shown promise in the prevention and treatment of cancer! Studies have proven that combining piperine and along with curcumin (the main pigment in turmeric) aids the absorption of curcumin into the bloodstream, protecting the body's cells from oxidative stress.

Detox Cure

4 servings

2 cups (500 ml) kale
1 cup (250 ml) water
1/2 avocado
1/2 banana

In a blender, or with a hand blender, purée all ingredients until smooth. Serve.

According to research, kale, like broccoli and other leafy greens, stops the growth of pre-cancerous cells thanks to the cancer-fighting sulforaphane it produces. Combine it with avocado in a smoothie for the ultimate detoxifying drink!

A.M. Turmeric

Orange Mandarin

1 serving

1/4 cup (60 ml) orange juice
4 mandarin oranges, seeded
1/2 cup (125 ml) plain probiotic yogurt
Crushed ice

In a blender, purée all ingredients until smooth. Serve.

Polyphenols and terpenes are the active ingredients in citrus fruits. Eating citrus fruit is an excellent way to incorporate anticancer foods into your diet.

Mango Papaya

4 servings

2 ripe papayas, peeled, seeded, and chopped
3/4 cup (180 ml) mango juice
Juice of **1** lime

In a blender, or with a hand blender, purée all ingredients until smooth. Serve.

Papaya is rich in antioxidants and chemical compounds, which help reduce the risk of cardiovascular diseases, certain types of cancer, and various chronic illnesses. Mango has powerful anticancer properties!

Probiotic Berry

2 servings

1/2 cup (125 ml) water
Juice of **1/2** lemon
1 cup (250 ml) berries of your choice
1-inch piece fresh ginger
1/2 cup (125 ml) plain probiotic yogurt

In a blender, or with a hand blender, purée all ingredients until smooth. Serve.

Try a mixture of strawberries, blackcurrants, cherries, blackberries, and blueberries. Replace the water with blueberry juice! To slow the development of tumors and help reduce inflammation, there is nothing better than berries! Their high level of polyphenolic compounds and bioactive phytochemicals fight cardiovascular diseases and cancer.

Pear and Broccoli

2 servings

4 pears, cored and cut into pieces
2 green apples, cored and cut into pieces
6 broccoli florets
2 kiwis, peeled and cut into pieces

There are two ways to prepare this smoothie:

1. Juice the ingredients in a juicer. Serve.

2. In a blender, or with a hand blender, purée all ingredients until smooth, except kiwis. Add kiwis and blend for 1 minute, adding water as needed. Serve.

Save your pear and apple peels: they contain precious cancer-fighting flavonoids and phenolic acids.

Broccoli stimulates the body's anticancer genes, and the antioxidants in kiwis help prevent cardiovascular diseases and certain cancers.

Smoothies for the Immune System

Eating well and seeking out specific vitamins is an excellent way to boost the immune system. In order to get through the cold months without a runny nose or a pesky scratch in your throat, a few small dietary changes can be introduced, starting with making fresh fruits and vegetables the number one foods in your diet.

Cold Remedy

1 orange
1/4 cup (60 ml) sweet melon or cantaloupe, chopped
1 or **2** slices fresh pineapple
7 blanched almonds or **1 tbsp** almond flour
1/4 cup (60 ml) probiotic yogurt
Crushed ice

In a blender, or with a hand blender, purée all ingredients until smooth. If mixture is too thick, add a bit of fresh orange juice. Serve immediately.

As everyone knows, oranges and pineapples are extremely rich in vitamin C, a powerful antioxidant that helps heal wounds and form scar tissue, and boosts the immune system. Melon provides vitamin A, and almonds supply vitamin E. As an added bonus, the probiotics in the yogurt restore essential intestinal flora.

The Energetic

1 serving

1/2 cup (125 ml) apple juice
1 pear, cored and cut into pieces
1 cup (250 ml) fresh or frozen strawberries
1/2 banana
1 tbsp maple syrup
Crushed ice

In a blender, purée all ingredients until smooth. Serve immediately.

Pears and strawberries are excellent sources of fiber and are also remineralizing. Bananas strengthen the immune system by preventing certain illnesses, such as the cold and the flu, thanks to their high concentration of the essential nutrient vitamin C. Apple juice, on the other hand, helps maintain the delicate balance of good and bad bacteria that live in the colon.

Cold Remedy

Green Tea and Strawberry

2 servings

1/3 cup (80 ml) Kukicha* or sencha green tea, chilled

1 cup (250 ml) fresh or frozen strawberries

1/2 cup (125 ml) plain soft tofu or plain soy milk

1 tbsp real maple syrup or cane syrup

Crushed ice (optional)

* To prepare this tea, infuse 1 1/2 tsp Kukicha tea leaves in 1 cup (250 ml) boiling water for 1 to 5 minutes.

In a blender, or with a hand blender, purée all ingredients until smooth. Add crushed ice if strawberries are fresh.

Soft tofu, also known as silken tofu, should be stored in water and will keep in the refrigerator for 7 to 10 days. Change the tofu water daily.

The vitamin C found in strawberries strengthens the immune system while acting as a powerful and effective antioxidant. One particular compound found in green tea is believed to play a key role in immune system health by increasing the number of certain beneficial cells. Soy is an excellent source of zinc, another nutrient responsible for the proper functioning of the immune system.

Immuniblues

1/2 cup (125 ml) fresh orange juice
1 cup (250 ml) frozen blueberries
1/2 banana
1 tbsp ground or powdered almonds
1 tsp almond butter

In a blender, or with a hand blender, purée all ingredients until smooth. Add more orange juice as needed. Serve.

Orange juice and blueberries contribute to strengthening the immune system and help reduce inflammation. Almonds are an excellent food for helping curb the appetite and, most importantly, they help lower cholesterol.

Cranberry Orange

3 servings

1 cup (250 ml) water
4 oranges, cut into pieces
3/4 cup (180 ml) fresh or frozen cranberries

In a blender, or with a hand blender, crush oranges. Slowly add cranberries and water, then purée until smooth. Serve.

A fitting autumn smoothie containing a massive dose of antioxidants and vitamin C, two nutrients that contribute to immune system health.

The Green Banana

2 servings

1 banana, cut into pieces
1-1/2 cups green grapes
1/2 apple, cut into pieces
1 cup (250 ml) baby spinach
1 cup (250 ml) plain yogurt

In a blender, or with a hand blender, purée all ingredients for 1 to 2 minutes, until smooth. If mixture is too thick, add a bit of soy milk. Serve immediately.

This smoothie will satisfy hunger and boost energy!

Orange Trio

2 servings

3/4 cup (180 ml) fresh orange juice
1/2 cup (125 ml) carrots, peeled and cut into pieces
2 mangoes, cut into pieces
2 slices mango, as garnish
Crushed ice

In a blender, or with a hand blender, blend the orange juice and the carrots until puréed. Add the two mangoes and the crushed ice and purée until smooth. Pour into glasses and garnish with a slice of mango. Serve immediately.

Rich in provitamin A and in beta-carotene, carrots and mangoes contain a considerable amount of antioxidant vitamins as well as a beneficial amount of dietary fiber. They also support the mechanisms that stimulate the immune system, while oranges provide vitamin C.

Pumpkin Potion

2 servings

Juice of **3** oranges, freshly pressed, or
1 cup (250 ml) orange juice
1 cup (250 ml) pumpkin, cooked*
1 apple, cored

* To cook the pumpkin, start by thoroughly washing
  it. Cut pumpkin in two and scoop out the seeds.
  Place, cut sides down, on an oiled baking sheet
  and cook in a 375 °F (190 °C) for 1 hour, or until
  tender. Let cool. Pumpkins are easier to cut into
  pieces and peel once cooked.

  The pumpkin seeds can be saved and eaten
  as a delicious snack! Just rinse and dry the seeds,
  and then drizzle with oil and sprinkle with salt.
  Cook in a 350 °F (175 °C) oven for 10 to 15 minutes,
  or until crispy.

In a blender, or with a hand blender, purée
all ingredients until smooth. Serve chilled.

The pumpkin is very rich in provitamin A (or beta-carotene), a major antioxidant that plays a role in preventing cancer, increasing immunity, and improving arteriosclerosis. In addition, the pumpkin is rich in inulin, a probiotic that stimulates the development of the intestinal flora. Pumpkin oil (very common in Austria) helps enlarge the prostate.

Winter squash and pumpkin are often mistaken for each other, the latter being more common in North America and Asia. The pumpkin has a round shape and is orange in color, whereas the winter squash, more common in Europe, is more or less flat and, depending on the variety, varies from red to dark green in color. Winter squash flesh has a more delicate flavor than pumpkin flesh.

Smoothies for Detoxing

Over time, the unhealthy substances and additives we consume and are exposed to build up in our systems, affecting overall health and causing fatigue, irritability, and depression, and decreasing the body's ability to fight infection. Detoxifying smoothies cleanse the body by removing impurities, helping us feel healthier and more energetic. However, as with any cleanse, commitment is key. It is important to limit, or even eliminate, obstacles to your healing process, including sugar, alcohol, tobacco, coffee, and refined products. Opt for natural and organic products, drink lots of water, be sure to get enough sleep, and try your best to maintain a healthy lifestyle, even after completing your cleanse.

Kiwi Banana

2 servings

3/4 cup (180 ml) carrot juice
1 tbsp dried goji berries
Juice of 1/2 lime
1 green apple, unpeeled, cored, and cut
into pieces
1 kiwi, peeled
1/2 cup (125 ml) fresh pineapple, peeled
and cut into pieces
1/2 banana

In a blender, soak goji berries for a few minutes in the carrot juice to rehydrate. Purée ingredients until smooth, adding them one at a time. Serve.

Kiwis have a diuretic effect and are rich in vitamin C. Vitamin C helps the body produce the antioxidant glutathione that binds to fat-soluble toxic compounds, making them water soluble and easily excreted from the body. Pineapple contains bromelain, which helps break down proteins in the gastrointestinal tract, while bananas contribute to a healthy excretory system.

Creamy Cherry

1 cup (250 ml) milk (oat, rice, or soy)
1 cup (250 ml) cherries, pitted
1/4 cup (60 ml) fresh pineapple, peeled and cut into pieces
1 cup (250 ml) plain yogurt

In a blender, or with a hand blender, purée all ingredients until smooth. Serve immediately.

Fresh cherries have a diuretic and mild laxative effect. Fresh pineapple has a high concentration of anti-inflammatory enzymes that improve intestinal function.

Apple, Avocado and Carrot

1 serving

1 green apple, cored and cut into pieces
1/2 cup (125 ml) carrot juice
1 avocado, cut into pieces
1 tsp fresh ginger, grated

Finely chop apple in a blender, or with a hand blender, and then add carrot juice. Add avocado and ginger and purée until smooth. Serve immediately.

Carrots hydrate the skin, improve vision, and relieve digestive problems. Apples are rich in quercetin and cholesterol-lowering vitamin C. Avocados, like kiwis, contain glutathione.

Cran-Beet

3 servings

1 cup (250 ml) cranberry juice
2 beets, cooked, peeled, and cubed
1/4 cup (60 ml) fresh or frozen raspberries
1 cup (250 ml) plain low-fat yogurt
A few raspberries for garnish (optional)

In a blender, or with a hand blender, purée all ingredients until smooth. Serve immediately.

The betanin in beets accelerates the breakdown of fatty acids in the liver, reducing stress on this vital organ and improving its ability to fight more harmful toxins. Cranberries have unique properties that help fight urinary tract infections and eliminate body waste.

Watercress, Apple and Cucumber Detox

2 servings

1 apple, unpeeled, cored, and diced
1 small cucumber, peeled and diced
1/2 bunch watercress
10 mint leaves
Crushed ice

In a blender, purée all ingredients until smooth. Serve immediately.

Watercress increases certain enzymes that stimulate detoxification.

Strawberry Grapefruit

1 grapefruit
1 cup (250 ml) fresh or frozen strawberries
1/2 fresh or frozen banana
7 or **8** leaves romaine lettuce, washed and dried

In a blender, or with a hand blender, purée all ingredients until smooth, except lettuce. Add lettuce and pulse until smooth.

Strawberries assist the liver in eliminating waste, are easy to digest, and are a good source of vitamins and minerals. Grapefruit flushes out toxins and is a natural remedy for water retention and bloating. It also improves blood circulation, stimulates weight loss, promotes healthy kidney function, and, best of all, is a natural antidepressant.

Maximum Detox

4 servings

1/3 cup (80 ml) grapefruit (or pomelo) juice
2 green apples, cored
1/2 cucumber, peeled and seeded
2 tbsp fresh ginger, roughly chopped
12 fresh mint leaves (**4** for garnish)
Crushed ice

In a blender, purée all ingredients until smooth. Garnish with mint leaves.

Cucumber is widely believed to have regenerative properties. Apples, rich in pectin and fiber, help flush out toxins and eliminate waste through the urine, while grapefruit has a natural laxative effect.

Smoothies for Vitality

There is no secret to increasing your vitality: the key is a healthy and balanced diet, combined with a healthy weight and regular exercise. A healthy lifestyle also reduces the risk of cancer. The best foods to eat are grain products that are high in fiber, as well as plenty of fruits and vegetables. A low-fat diet should be adopted: switch to leaner meats and prepared foods that are also low in fat. Alcohol presents health risks and should be consumed in limited amounts. Vitamins E, C, and A, as well as the beta-carotene present in fruits and vegetables, are powerful antioxidants that help fight free radicals and cancer.

Bok Choy and Peaches

1/4 **cup (60 ml)** water
1 cup (250 ml) baby bok choy, chopped
1/2 fresh or frozen banana
1 peach, cut into pieces
Crushed ice

In a blender, purée all ingredients until smooth. Serve immediately.

One tablespoon of bok choy contains less than 20 calories and provides 144% of the recommended daily intake of vitamin A, as well a good portion of the recommended daily intake of vitamin C. It also contains calcium, magnesium, potassium, and folate. The peach, on the other hand, is a widely known digestive aid. It is rich in vitamin A, which is concentrated in its skin, so it is best not to peel it.

Mango Pineapple

1 serving

1 mango, cut into pieces
2 large pineapple rings, peeled
Crushed ice

In a blender, purée all ingredients until smooth. If mixture is too thick, add a bit of water or orange juice.

Mango is an excellent source of provitamin A, a great brain cell protector that prevents age-related damage, and an ally in reducing the risk of heart attacks and strokes. This provitamin also encourages the healing of wounds and cuts, and protects skin against harmful environmental factors, such as the sun.

Energy +

1 red apple, cored and quartered
1 carrot, peeled and cut into pieces
1 beet, cooked
1 cup (250 ml) baby spinach
1 sprig fresh dill

In a blender, or with a hand blender, combine all ingredients, starting with the apple, and purée until smooth. If mixture is too thick, add a bit of water.

If you are overtired, this smoothie will supply you with a burst of energy! Rich in fiber, it helps regulate blood sugar levels, providing energy and a feeling of well-being. Spinach promotes hormonal balance, and beets encourage healthy digestion.

Life Cocktail

1 serving

1 cup (250 ml) orange juice
2 or **3** carrots, peeled and cut into small pieces
1 stalk celery, coarsely chopped
1 tsp sesame seeds

In a blender, or with a hand blender, purée all ingredients until relatively smooth. Strain the purée to make it smoother, if desired.

This is a great cocktail to boost and balance the body's defenses, while also providing energy to start the day on the right foot! Carrots and oranges give the skin a beautiful glow, and celery is an excellent diuretic. Carotenoids are a natural shield against the effects of aging skin.

Soyapricot

2 servings

1 cup (250 ml) soy milk
Crushed ice
8 fresh apricots, pitted and cut into pieces
2 pinches ground black pepper
1 tbsp sesame seeds
1 slice (round) lemon
1/2 tsp fresh thyme leaves, chopped
1 tsp sesame seeds

In a blender, or with a hand blender, purée soy milk, crushed ice, apricots, ground pepper, and 1 tbsp sesame seeds until smooth. Combine sesame seeds and thyme. To prepare glasses, coat the rims with lemon juice, and then dip them in sesame seed and thyme mixture. Pour smoothie into glasses and garnish with fresh thyme.

The more intense the color of the apricot, the richer it is in provitamin A (or beta-carotene), which protects cells against free radicals thanks to its antioxidant properties. This provitamin also plays an important role in skin health by regulating the growth of skin cells and improving epidermal collagen levels. Sesame's sesamin increases the amount of vitamin E available in the blood and tissues, which helps reduce inflammation. It acts in synergy with vitamin C and carotenoids, reinforcing their protective action. It is also involved in the body's protection against ultraviolet B radiation.

Superman GO!

4 oranges
1/2 lime
1 mango, cut into pieces
3 tbsp plain yogurt

Press oranges and lime with a citrus press. In a blender, or with a hand blender, purée all ingredients until smooth. Drink fresh!

Mango and orange are excellent sources of vitamins to kick-start the day; lime is a powerful antiseptic.

Smoothies for Menopause

These smoothies are often made with soy milk, which is rich in phytoestrogens: naturally-occurring plant compounds similar to female estrogen hormones that have many potential health benefits. And of course, fruit is loaded with vitamins and nutrients!

Cholesterol Blaster!

Cholesterol Blaster!

1 serving

1/2 cup (125 ml) pomegranate juice
1/2 cup (125 ml) frozen strawberries
1/2 cup (125 ml) frozen blueberries

In a blender, or with a hand blender, purée all ingredients until smooth. Drink immediately. If desired, add raspberries or blackberries, and for extra creaminess, pour in 1/2 cup (125 ml) soy milk.

Women's cholesterol levels rise sharply around menopause, increasing the risk of various diseases. Pomegranate juice, as well as berries, are high in anthocyanins and help lower cholesterol levels.

Raspberry Banana

1 serving

1/2 cup (125 ml) almond milk
1 cup (250 ml) frozen raspberries
1/2 banana
1 tbsp flaxseeds

In a blender, or with a hand blender, purée all ingredients until smooth. Top with a few fresh raspberries and serve.

Store fresh, whole flaxseeds in the freezer for up to one month. Or, for everyday use, grind a smaller amount once a week and store in the freezer in an airtight, opaque container.

Almond milk is an excellent source of calcium, magnesium, potassium, phosphorus, and essential fatty acids. Gluten free and rich in fiber and protein, this milk is a superior source of antioxidant vitamin E and protects against cell and skin aging. To increase phytoestrogen intake, replace the almond milk in this smoothie with the same quantity of soy milk. Flaxseeds are high in omega-3 fatty acids, fiber, and phytoestrogens, all of which help control menopause symptoms.

Cranberry, Pear and Strawberry

3 servings

1/2 cup (125 ml) fresh or frozen cranberries
3 pears, unpeeled and cored
1-1/2 cups (375 ml) fresh or frozen strawberries
Crushed ice

In a blender, purée all ingredients until smooth. If mixture is too thick, add a bit of water, pear juice, or cranberry juice. Serve immediately.

If desired, substitute 1/2 cup (125 ml) pure cranberry juice for the fresh or frozen cranberries.

Cranberries are the best natural remedy for urinary tract infections, which occur frequently during menopause, and they also help lower cholesterol levels. The boron in pears raises estrogen levels in menopausal women, and strawberries contain beneficial antioxidant properties.

Fruitsation

2 cups (500 ml) soy milk
1 large fresh or frozen banana

Add **2** of the following:
1 mango, cut into pieces
2 kiwis, peeled
2 apricots, pitted
1/2 cup (125 ml) frozen raspberries
or strawberries
1 peach or nectarine, peeled and pitted
1 or **2** slices fresh pineapple, peeled
3 plums, pitted

Crushed ice

In a blender, purée all ingredients until smooth. Serve immediately.

Pure Purple

2 tbsp ground flaxseeds
1 cup (250 ml) frozen blueberries, blackberries, or blackcurrants
10 fresh or frozen strawberries
1/2 banana
1/2 cup (125 ml) low-fat yogurt (Greek or Balkan-style)
1/4 cup (60 ml) low-fat milk or soy milk

In a blender, or with a hand blender, purée all ingredients until smooth. If the mixture is too thick, add a bit of low-fat milk or soy milk. Serve immediately.

This smoothie is a drinkable fountain of youth for women over 50! The berries it contains lower cholesterol, flaxseeds provide phytoestrogen, and yogurt promotes healthy bones.

Fruitsation

Smoothies for Andropause

Andropause, or male menopause, is a stage of aging in a man's life that typically begins around age 40, marked by both physical and psychological changes. Decreasing levels of testosterone may cause a variety of symptoms including reduced energy and vitality, a decrease in libido and sexual function, fatigue, trouble sleeping, anxiety, and depression.

Asparagus and Chervil

2 servings

10 asparagus stalks
1-1/2 cups (375 ml) chicken stock
1/4 cup (60 ml) cream (any kind)
1/2 bunch fresh chervil, chopped
Salt and pepper
Crushed ice

In a large pot, bring chicken stock to a boil and cook asparagus. Let cool.

In a blender, or with a hand blender, purée asparagus, cream, and chervil until smooth. Season with salt and pepper and add crushed ice. Serve.

Fresh chervil possesses diuretic properties.

Testosterone Boost

2 servings

10 dates, pitted
1/2 cup (125 ml) coconut water
1/2 avocado
2 bananas, cut into rounds
3 celery stalks, chopped
Crushed ice

In a blender, purée dates with coconut water. Add avocado, bananas, and celery, and blend together. Add crushed ice and purée until smooth and creamy. Serve.

Avocado is high in both folate, which helps metabolize proteins, and vitamin B6, which increases the production of male hormones.

The riboflavin in bananas also contributes to testosterone production, while fresh celery promotes testosterone production and stimulates the secretion of androsterone, a powerful male hormone released through the sweat glands as a pheromone; the body's natural aphrodisiac.

Asparagus and Chervil

Prostate Protective Smoothie

1/4 cup (60 ml) orange juice
1/2 cup fresh strawberries
1/2 banana, cut into pieces
3 tbsp yogurt (Balkan-style)
1 tbsp ground flaxseeds
2 tbsp pumpkin seeds, shelled
2 tbsp powdered whey protein
Crushed ice

In a blender, purée all ingredients until smooth and creamy. Serve.

Pumpkin seeds are a reputed health-boosting food, and are especially well known for helping to maintain a healthy prostate! These tasty seeds contain nutrients that promote testosterone production, and are extremely rich in zinc, an essential element for healthy sex organs.

Good-for-You Grapes

1-1/2 cups (375 ml) grape juice
1/2 cup (125 ml) plain yogurt
1 banana

In a blender, or with a hand blender, purée all ingredients for 30 to 60 seconds until smooth and creamy.

The flavonoids in grapes that give them their red color are also protective pigments with powerful cellular antioxidant activity, which helps slow the effects of aging and promote the regeneration of the cardiovascular system. Because these antioxidants bind to the collagen in the arterial walls, they help strengthen and increase flexibility in the arteries as well as the veins and capillaries. They also encourage vasodilation, a process that widens the blood vessels in the penis, necessary to produce and maintain an erection.

Asparagus

1 serving

1/2 cup (125 ml) cream, heated
4 asparagus stalks, steamed
1 green zucchini, peeled and cooked
A few rosemary leaves

In a blender, or with a hand blender, purée all ingredients until smooth. Serve.

This smoothie can also be served as an appetizer! Asparagus is rich in steroids, and phytoestrogens in particular, which also stimulate testosterone production.

Good-for-You Grapes

Smoothies for the Nervous System

Studies have proven that most cases of severe depression, bipolar disorder, postpartum depression, and anger-related issues are associated with a diet low in omega-3 fatty acids. To prevent omega-3 deficiency, eat foods like spinach and flaxseed oil.

Anti-Stress Smoothie

2 servings

1 cup (250 ml) lemon balm infusion*, chilled
1 cup (250 ml) frozen blueberries
1/2 or **1** whole frozen banana, or 2 large slices
fresh pineapple
1 cup (250 ml) baby spinach
1 tbsp almond butter
1 tbsp flaxseed oil

* To prepare the lemon balm infusion, boil 1 cup
water and add 1 tsp dried lemon balm leaves.
Let steep, and then chill. If desired, chill the
infusion in an ice cube tray and use in your drinks
and smoothies. You can also substitute the
infusion with almond milk or plain yogurt.

In a blender, or with a hand blender, purée
all ingredients until smooth. Serve.

Blueberries provide vitamin C, as well as potassium, which keeps the nervous system functioning optimally. Bananas are high in calming B vitamins, and fresh pineapple is rich in calcium. Spinach is a good source of folate, vitamin B6, iron, potassium, and magnesium, which are all essential nutrients that help combat stress. Almonds are rich in vitamin E and calcium, and help lower cholesterol, while lemon balm strengthens the nervous system.

Blueberry Oat Delight

1 to 2 servings

1/2 cup (125 ml) oat milk

1-1/2 cups (375 ml) frozen blueberries

3 small very ripe kiwis, peeled and sliced

1 frozen banana

3 to **5** fresh or dried dates, pitted

2/3 cup (160 ml) oats

* Rehydrate dried dates by soaking them in 1/2 cup boiling water for 5 minutes. Drain and chop before adding to your smoothie.

In a blender, or with a hand blender, purée all ingredients until smooth. This smoothie will be quite thick, and is easier to eat with a spoon. If desired, add a bit of oat milk or water to thin it out.

Oats are a natural nerve relaxant. They contain phosphorus, calcium, zinc, magnesium, B vitamins, avenin, and carbohydrates, are low in fat, and help strengthen and balance the nervous system.

B Vitamin Burst

4 servings

1 cup (250 ml) water
3 ripe pears, unpeeled, cored and cut
into pieces
1 cup (250 ml) mâche (also called lamb's
lettuce or corn salad)
2 cups (500 ml) spinach
1 tsp mesquite powder
1 pinch cinnamon

In a blender, or with a hand blender,
purée all ingredients until smooth.
Serve immediately.

All eight B-group vitamins play a key role in many of the chemical reactions in the body, especially in the reactions that take place in the nervous system. Vitamins B9 and B12 are the primary vitamins in the proper functioning of the nervous system, and vitamin B9 (also known as folate), in particular, is an essential element in neural communication. Mâche, rich in omega-3s, is a very good source of vitamin B9, as is spinach.

Chocoberry Smoothie

1 to 2 servings

1 cup (250 ml) almond milk
1 tbsp goji berries
1 tsp chia seeds
1 tbsp flaxseed oil
1 cup (250 ml) fresh or frozen raspberries
1/4 cup (60 ml) fresh or frozen blackberries
1 tbsp cocoa powder
1 tsp real maple syrup
Crushed ice (optional)

In a blender, soak goji berries in the almond milk for 5 minutes to rehydrate. Add remaining ingredients and purée until smooth. If fruit is fresh, add crushed ice. Serve immediately.

Cocoa, seeds, nuts, and almonds are all rich in magnesium, a mineral that promotes neuroplasticity, improves memory, and helps fight stress.

Smoothies for Digestion

Fruit and vegetable juices are liquid gold when it comes to bioavailable nutrients. Unlike solid foods, juices require hardly any energy to digest, so the body can absorb these nutrients much more quickly, which speeds up the cleansing process. Starting off with a piece of fruit, or some fresh-cut raw vegetables, is a great way to eat less during a meal.

Pineapple, Papaya and Ginger

2 servings

1 small papaya, peeled and seeded
2 large slices fresh pineapple
1 container **(6 oz)** plain yogurt
1-inch piece fresh ginger, peeled
Crushed ice

In a blender, purée all ingredients until smooth. Serve.

The bromelain in pineapple and the papain in papaya are enzymes that facilitate digestion; ginger stimulates bile secretion, as well as various different digestive enzymes.

Peachy Almond Smoothie

2 servings

3/4 to **1 cup (180 to 250 ml)** almond milk
2 or **3** peaches, pitted
1 tbsp honey
Crushed ice

In a blender, purée all ingredients until smooth. Serve.

Great for digestion and intestinal transit, peaches are a juicy, delicious treat. If they are pesticide free, they should be eaten with the skin, as the skin carries many essential nutrients.

...nd *Smoothie*

2 servings

In a blender, combine blackcurrants, blackberries, oranges, and ginger. Add ice and purée until smooth. Serve immediately.

...nal system and stimulate the liver and ...people suffering from gastrointestinal ...production of gastric juices when eaten ...all red berries, are rich in flavonoids, ...hich contribute to maintaining a healthy

Kiwi, Green Apple, Grape and Pineapple

1 serving

1 green apple, cored and quartered
1 kiwi, peeled
10 grapes, halved
1 large slice fresh pineapple, peeled

In a blender, or with a hand blender, purée ingredients, starting with the apple. Add kiwi, grapes, and pineapple. Drink immediately.

Drink this smoothie before eating meat, or in the morning, after a heavy meal the night before. Kiwis and pineapples contain enzymes that ease digestion, while the apple's dietary fiber helps food move through the intestines and absorb vital nutrients.

Apple Pear

2 servings

1 cup (250 ml) fresh apple juice (not from concentrate)
1 or **2** pears, unpeeled and cored
1/2 tsp vanilla extract or 1 packet vanilla sugar
A few drops lemon juice

In a blender, or with a hand blender, purée all ingredients until smooth. Serve immediately.

Composed of 84% water, pears possess laxative and diuretic properties and help soothe sore stomachs. People suffering from digestive problems should choose pears with a soft, creamy texture over those with grittier, grainy flesh. The best time to eat a pear is after a meal, since its deliciously sweet taste will satisfy your sweet tooth and the sugars will provide extra energy.

Papaya and Passion Fruit

2 servings

1 cup (250 ml) orange juice
1 papaya, peeled and seeded
2 passion fruits, seeds only
Crushed ice

In a blender, purée all ingredients until smooth. Serve immediately.

Papaya contains papain, an enzyme that facilitates digestion and soothes an upset stomach, while passion fruit helps prevent constipation. A fiber-rich diet lowers the risk of colon cancer, and offsets hunger by increasing the feeling of fullness.

Pre-Dinner Cocktail Smoothie

1 serving

1 tsp cider or apple juice
1/4 cup (60 ml) grape juice
1 slice fresh pineapple, peeled
1/2 red bell pepper
1/4 cup (60 ml) plain yogurt
1 pinch ground ginger
Crushed ice

In a blender, purée all ingredients until smooth. Serve.

Pineapple stimulates gastric secretions, while red pepper is an excellent source of vitamin C and carotene, as well as flavonoids, which act as an antioxidant and help prevent the premature aging of cells.

Smoothies for Headaches

Poor diet is often to blame for headaches and migraines, which can be triggered by high-fat meals or too much meat, coffee (or quitting coffee cold turkey), wine, chocolate, MSG, cheese, ice cream, etc. Migraine sufferers should identify trigger foods and practice healthy dietary habits to help keep headaches away.

Dried Apricot and Banana

1 serving

1/2 cup (125 ml) almond milk
1/2 fresh or frozen banana
4 dried apricots
1 tbsp lemon juice

In a blender, or with a hand blender, purée all ingredients until smooth.

Certain experts believe that a diet rich in magnesium can help fight headaches. Some magnesium-rich foods include bananas, dates, dried apricots, avocados, almonds, and cashews.

Watermelon Raspberry

2 servings

1 cup (250 ml) watermelon, seeded
and chopped
1 cup (250 ml) raspberries
1 cup (250 ml) cold water
2 fresh mint leaves
Zest of **1/4** lemon
Crushed ice

In a blender, purée all ingredients until
smooth. If desired, add a bit more cold water.
Serve.

Dehydration is one of the most common causes of headaches. Be sure
to include plenty of water-rich foods in your diet, such as watermelon,
cucumber, tomato, and lettuce.

Avocado and Soy Milk

1 serving

1/2 cup (125 ml) soy milk
1 avocado, cut into pieces
1 tbsp flaxseed oil
Crushed ice

In a blender, purée all ingredients until
smooth. If mixture is too thick, add a bit
of soy milk. Drink immediately.

Headaches are often caused by dehydration, so it is important to rehydrate
the body, and especially the brain, by drinking water and pure fruit juices
(apple, orange, grape, pineapple, etc.). Hypoglycemia is also a common
culprit, so eating whole grains and nuts can also help prevent headaches.
In addition, the omega-3s in avocado, soy, and flax help keep brain
signals running smoothly.

Banana Cherry

1 serving

1/4 cup (60 ml) almond milk
1 cup (250 ml) cherries, pitted
1/2 banana, cut into pieces
Juice of 1/2 lemon
Crushed ice

In a blender, purée all ingredients until smooth. Serve.

Researchers have found that the anthocyanins found in cherries act as a powerful antioxidant and anti-inflammatory, and eating just 20 cherries has been shown to relieve the pain associated with headaches.

Date Smoothie

1 serving

1/4 cup (60 ml) orange juice
1/2 cup (125 ml) almond milk
4 dates, pitted and chopped
1/2 banana
Crushed ice

In a blender, purée all ingredients until smooth. Serve.

During a migraine, the blood vessels in the brain become constricted, so avoiding products that cause blood vessel contraction is strongly recommended. Instead, drink green tea and plenty of water, and choose magnesium-rich foods. Because magnesium is a natural relaxant and stress reliever, it has positive effects on the nervous and circulatory systems: it is the trace mineral essential for nerve impulse transmission, energy production, muscle contraction, and stress regulation.

Smoothies for Insomnia and Sleep Disorders

Melatonin, often called "the sleep hormone," is released by the body at night and is responsible for maintaining the body's natural biorhythm. It also functions as a powerful antioxidant, enabling it to protect against cell oxidation and aging. When melatonin production is disrupted, it can cause insomnia and a variety of other sleeping problems.

Morpheus, God of Dreams

Morpheus, God of Dreams

1 serving

1/2 **cup (125 ml)** oat milk
1/2 **cup (125 ml)** plain yogurt (Balkan-style)
1/2 banana
3 **tbsp** oats

In a blender, or with a hand blender, purée all ingredients until smooth. Drink before bedtime.

Warning: Oats are not recommended for people who are following a gluten-free diet. Oats contain tryptophan, an amino acid essential to protein production. Tryptophan also helps control the appetite and regulates the sleep cycle, as well as the mood. Just one cup of cooked oatmeal provides 25% of the recommended daily intake.

Sweet Dreams

1 serving

1 banana
1 mango, cut into pieces
1 mâche lettuce (also called lamb's lettuce or corn salad)

In a blender, or with a hand blender, purée all ingredients until smooth. If desired, add a bit of water. Serve.

Omega-3 fatty acids slow the production of the prostaglandin E2. When the body produces too much of this prostaglandin, it can accelerate neuronal aging and affect the transmission of chemical messages in the brain, which can disrupt normal sleeping patterns. Mâche is a natural plant source of essential fatty acids and provides a significant amount of the recommended daily intake.

Hazelnut Almond

13 hazelnuts, blanched
3 tbsp ground almonds
1 cup (250 ml) 2% milk
1 tbsp real maple syrup

Mix together hazelnuts, ground almonds, and milk. Refrigerate for 4 hours.

In a blender, or with a hand blender, purée all ingredients until smooth. Serve.

Nuts are a good source of melatonin and contain vitamin E, which helps keep the heart, brain, muscles, joints, eyes, skin, digestive system, and immune system healthy.

Goodbye Jet Lag

1 apple, cored and cut into pieces
3 or **4** leaves curly cabbage (such as kale)
1 carrot, peeled and chopped
1 small bunch parsley
10 to **20** fresh pumpkin seeds, hulled, or
1 tbsp pumpkin seed oil

In a blender, or with a hand blender, purée all ingredients until smooth. If desired, add a bit of water. Serve.

Drinking this smoothie 30 minutes before bedtime is an effective treatment for sleeping problems caused by jet lag. Curly cabbage is packed with detoxifying nutrients and helps the body to relax, carrots and apples also act as relaxants, and balance the level of sugar in the blood. Pumpkin seeds are high in tryptophan, an amino acid that acts as a biochemical precursor for the sleep-regulating hormone melatonin.

Hazelnut Almond

163

Tasty Tomato

4 tomatoes, peeled and chopped
1 shallot, finely chopped
1/2 cup (125 ml) oat milk
1/2 cup (125 ml) plain yogurt (Balkan-style)
A few fresh basil leaves
Salt and freshly ground pepper

In a blender, or with a hand blender, pulse together tomatoes and shallot. Gradually pour in oat milk, and then add yogurt and basil. Purée until smooth. Garnish with a few more basil leaves.

The easiest way to peel tomatoes is to plunge them in boiling water for 30 seconds before peeling.

Insomnia-fighting foods containing melatonin (or tryptophan) include bananas, tomatoes, ginger, rice, corn, oats, barley, and nuts.

Smoothies for Longevity

Life expectancy and quality of life can be increased with simple steps and changes, and maintaining a healthy diet is an essential factor in any long-term lifestyle goals. Scientific studies have shown that consuming five to ten servings a day of fruits and vegetables significantly reduces the risk of heart disease and certain types of cancer, and helps prevent hypertension and hypercholesterolemia. Fruits and vegetables, especially dark green and orange fruits and vegetables, contain health-giving vitamins and minerals that help the body fight infections and certain illnesses. People from the Okinawa region of Japan have a life expectancy among the highest in the world, and often reach 100 years of age, or older. This long lifespan is attributed to a diet rich in algae, green tea, and vegetable proteins, and to lifestyle and environmental factors, including physical activity.

Liquid Youth

4 cups water

2 leaves Chinese cabbage, shredded

1 baby bok choy

2 large broccoli florets

1 carrot, peeled and cut into pieces

1 zucchini (green or yellow), unpeeled

1 cup (250 ml) mixed berries

In a blender, or with a hand blender, purée all ingredients until smooth. Drink for breakfast.

When eaten regularly, cruciferous vegetables (cabbage, broccoli, cauliflower, Chinese cabbage, kale, etc.) help prevent different types of cancer, including cancers of the lungs, pancreas, ovaries, and kidneys.

Eternal Youth

1 serving

2 tbsp grape juice

15 fresh or frozen blueberries

10 fresh or frozen strawberries

1/2 apple, unpeeled

8 cranberries

5 acerola or sour cherries, pitted

5 aronia berries (chokeberries) or

2 tbsp aronia berry juice

In a blender, or with a hand blender, purée all ingredients until smooth. Drink immediately.

Aronia berry juice has antioxidant properties, regulates arterial tension, and helps slow the effects of aging as well as prevent complications in diabetes patients. Cranberries and cherries are widely praised for their therapeutic effects and their exceptionally high concentration of antioxidants.

Vitality Cocktail

1 cup (250 ml) berries of your choice
1/2 cup (125 ml) probiotic yogurt
1/4 cup (60 ml) ground almonds
1 tsp canola oil
1 tbsp flaxseeds, freshly ground
1 tbsp brewer's yeast
Crushed ice

In a blender, purée all ingredients until smooth. Drink immediately.

Probiotics boost the immune system, and brewer's yeast contains a number of essential nutrients, most notably vitamins B and D. It also contains 46% of the recommended daily intake of protein, as well as mineral salts, trace elements, and amino acids.

Zen Breakfast

1 cup (250 ml) soy milk
1 avocado
1 tbsp honey
1/4 tsp cinnamon

In a blender, or with a hand blender, purée all ingredients until smooth. Drink for breakfast.

Honey and cinnamon are powerful antioxidants and are widely praised for their healing properties.

Regeneration

1 kiwi
1 cup (250 ml) vanilla probiotic yogurt
1 tsp green tea extract
1/4 cup (60 ml) wheatgrass powder
1 tbsp canola oil
1 tbsp flaxseed, freshly ground
1 tbsp honey
Crushed ice

In a blender, purée all ingredients until smooth. Drink immediately.

The antioxidant effect of green tea is 200 times more powerful than that of vitamin E. Wheatgrass powder fortifies the immune system and is rich in minerals, vitamins, proteins, and enzymes. It also contains chlorophyll, which flushes out accumulated toxins and helps cleanse the liver, lungs, and colon.

Smoothies to Fight Wrinkles

As the body ages, the skin weakens and starts to loosen and sag. But rest assured, it is possible to slow the signs of aging! Exposure to sun, pollution, and cigarette smoke activates oxidative damage that can actually be neutralized by certain antioxidants. By choosing foods that are rich in antioxidants, we are protecting our skin against the wear and tear of daily life and helping it age better. Fruit contains antioxidants and protects against the sun's free radicals. Filling your plate with fruit is also important for general good health, and a healthy person has healthy skin!

Citrus Smoothie

1 orange, peeled and pitted, pith
and membranes removed
1 pink or white grapefruit, peeled and pitted,
pith and membranes removed
1/2 cup (125 ml) skim milk
1/4 cup (60 ml) plain yogurt
2 tbsp lemon juice
1 tbsp cane syrup

In a blender, or with a hand blender, purée
all ingredients until smooth and creamy.
Serve.

All fruit is good for the skin, citrus fruit in particular. The vitamin C in citrus fruit helps produce collagen in the skin and improves microcirculation, brightening the skin instantly.

Grapefruit Ginger

2 servings

2 pink grapefruits, peeled and quartered
1/2 cup (125 ml) strawberries
1/2 banana, cut into rounds
1/2 cup (125 ml) almond milk
1-inch piece ginger, peeled and diced
A few mint leaves

In a blender, or with a hand blender, purée all ingredients until smooth. Garnish with mint leaves. Serve.

In general, we do not get enough selenium in our diets, and selenium plays a fundamental role in fighting cell-harming free radicals. Free radicals contribute to aging and weaken the body's ability to fight various viruses. Both grapefruits and almonds contain selenium.

Mango Pineapple

2 servings

1 mango, cut into pieces
1 pineapple, peeled and cut into pieces
2 bananas, cut into rounds
1 cup (250 ml) coconut milk (or light cream)
1 tbsp wheat protein

In a blender, or with a hand blender, purée all ingredients, except wheat protein, for 45 seconds, until mixture is smooth. Stir in wheat protein and serve.

The juice and flesh of fresh pineapple contains manganese, which helps fight free radicals, while mango is rich in beta-carotene and helps prevent premature cellular aging.

The Trio

Juice of **2** oranges, freshly pressed
Juice of **1/2** lime
6 strawberries
1 kiwi, peeled and cut into pieces

In a blender, or with a hand blender, purée all ingredients until smooth. Serve.

The kiwi is a superfood — it contains close to 20 essential nutrients! Its vitamin C content is five times greater than the orange and contains two times more vitamin E than the avocado. Vitamin C contributes to the production of collagen, which reduces wrinkles and protects skin from the harmful effects of the sun, as does vitamin E.

Kiwi Apricot

1 serving

1 kiwi, peeled and cut into pieces
2 fresh apricots, unpeeled, pitted
1/2 cup (125 ml) apple juice
1/2 cup (125 ml) plain yogurt (Balkan-style)
1 tbsp wheat germ
1 tbsp cane syrup

In a blender, or with a hand blender, purée all ingredients until smooth. Serve.

Vitamin E (tocopherol) is a powerful antioxidant that promotes cell regeneration and protects the lipids present in cell membranes. Vitamin E can be found in hazelnuts, wheat germ, grapeseed oil, kiwis, and apricots, amongst other foods. The average total content of carotenoids found in apricot skin is two to three times greater than in apricot flesh, making it an excellent source of beta-carotene.

Smoothies for a Flat Stomach

Cellulite is essentially fat deposits that accumulate mainly on the thighs, buttocks, and stomach. The ovaries are responsible for these deposits: the more estrogen they secrete, the more the fat cells (adipocytes) grow and multiply. To try and avoid cellulite, it is important to expend energy and be physically active. In order for the body to work anaerobically and to burn fat, practice endurance sports (like speed walking, jogging, cycling, and swimming), curb salt and sugar intake, and eat smaller portions. Foods that promote a flat stomach are those that are rich in monounsaturated fats (like avocados, flaxseed oil, and macadamia nuts), which have the capacity to change your physique by targeting tummy fat, the hardest fat to lose. A flat stomach is also a stomach that digests properly, so be sure to incorporate dietary fiber into your diet to improve intestinal transit.

Broccoli

2 or **3** broccoli florets, cooked al dente
1/2 cup (125 ml) plain yogurt
2 tsp maple syrup
1 tsp salt
Pepper

In a blender, or with a hand blender, purée all ingredients until smooth. If mixture is too thick, thin it with a bit of water.

Broccoli, in the cruciferous family (cabbage, kale, Brussels sprouts, spinach, cauliflower), is a detoxifying food, and can be eaten in large quantities without any worry about weight gain. It contains both vitamin C and sulfurous derivatives that help eliminate toxins from the liver.

Avocado and Citrus

1 serving

1 avocado, cut into pieces
1 fresh or frozen banana
1/2 cup (125 ml) orange juice
1/3 cup (80 ml) lime juice
1 tbsp cane syrup

In a blender, or with a hand blender, purée all ingredients until smooth. Serve immediately.

The fruits and vegetables highest in fiber are broccoli, potatoes, carrots, white cabbage, artichokes, dates, dried figs, apples, pears, almonds, avocados, bananas, pineapples, and apricots. Avocados are a great source of monounsaturated fats, which contain beta-sitosterols, natural phytosterols that fight cholesterol.

Apple Celery

2 servings

1/2 cup (125 ml) apple juice or water
Juice of **1** lemon
3 red apples, cored and cut into pieces
1 fresh or frozen banana
Heart of **1** small celery, coarsely chopped

In a blender, or with a hand blender, purée all ingredients until smooth. Serve immediately.

Celery helps reduce water retention and cellulite while improving bowel health and is said to limit the amount of fat absorbed by the cells.

Blood Orange and Pineapple

1 serving

1/2 pineapple, peeled and cut into pieces
Juice of **1/2** lime
2 blood oranges
1 tbsp cane syrup
Crushed ice

In a blender, purée all ingredients until smooth. Serve immediately.

The blood orange has a distinctive red flesh thanks to one particular pigment it contains: anthocyanin, which is present in many fruits but rare in citrus, and improves blood circulation. Blood oranges are also stocked with plenty of pectin. Concentrated in the white skin between the flesh and the peel, pectin promotes bowel health.

Apple

2 servings

1/2 cup (125 ml) apple juice
2 apples, cored and cut into pieces
1 fresh or frozen banana
3 Medjool dates, pitted and chopped
1/2 tsp ground cinnamon

In a blender, or with a hand blender, purée all ingredients until smooth. Add a bit of apple juice if mixture is too thick.

Apple's pectin forms a gel in the digestive tract that traps fats, limiting their absorption. Furthermore, pectin provides a feeling of fullness, regulates bowel health, and helps reduce bloating.

Peach Yogurt

1 serving

1/2 cup (125 ml) probiotic yogurt
1 fresh or frozen peach, pitted
Crushed ice

In a blender, purée all ingredients until smooth. Drink immediately.

Highly digestible and excellent for the intestinal flora, bifidus yogurt helps reduce stomach bloating and gives the waistline more definition in a matter of days.

Smoothies for "Heavy Leg" Syndrome

Many women suffer from "heavy leg" syndrome and associated leg conditions, including varicose veins and poor blood circulation, and the foods we eat play a vital role in the treatment of these conditions. The vitamins and antioxidants in fruits and vegetables strengthen and protect the veins, while the fiber they provide improves intestinal function, which, in turn, helps prevent venous stasis (slow blood flow in the veins, usually occurring in the legs). Drinking plenty of water flushes out toxins that have accumulated in swollen blood vessels; vitamin PP, found in raspberries, blackcurrants, blueberries and other berries, reduces water retention in the legs. Alcohol and cigarettes dilate the veins, and should be avoided; instead of coffee, which can intensify the symptoms of "heavy leg" syndrome, drink green tea to help strengthen the blood vessel walls.

Lighter Legs

2 cups (500 ml) watermelon, seeded and cut into pieces
1/2 cup (125 ml) apple juice
6 tbsp lemon juice
Zest of 1 lemon
1/2 cup (125 ml) sodium-free sparkling water

In a blender, or with a hand blender, purée all ingredients, except sparkling water, until smooth. Pour in sparkling water and mix with a spoon. Drink immediately.

Watermelon is loaded with antioxidants (lycopene, carotenoids, and vitamin C) that boost blood circulation, and the vitamin C it contains plays a vital role in collagen production.

Green Tea and Mango

2 servings

Juice of **2** oranges, freshly pressed, or
1/2 cup (125 ml) orange juice
1-1/2 cups (375 ml) green tea*
2 mangoes, cut into pieces
2 bananas, cut into rounds

* To prepare green tea, infuse 3 tbsp Kukicha tea
  leaves in 1-1/2 cups (375 ml) boiling water for
  1 to 5 minutes.

In a blender, or with a hand blender,
purée all ingredients until smooth.
Serve immediately.

Red berries, broccoli, spinach, cabbage, green tea, and the skin of fruits such as grapes, all contain a high concentration of flavonoids, which stimulate vein contraction, strengthen blood vessel walls, and thin the blood.

Pineapple and Black Grape

1 serving

1 cup (250 ml) fresh pineapple, peeled
and chopped
1/2 cup (125 ml) black grapes, with seeds
1/4 cup (60 ml) fresh or frozen
raspberries

In a blender*, or with a hand blender,
pulse all ingredients until smooth. Drink
immediately.

* Juicer instructions: Put all ingredients
  in the juicer, juice, and drink immediately.

This smoothie is bursting with fruits that are rich in vitamin P (anthocyanins and polyphenols). This vitamin promotes drainage and improves blood circulation and skin elasticity, making the legs feel lighter and revitalized.

Smoothie for Circulation

2 servings

Juice of **1** orange
1 carrot, peeled and cut into pieces
1/4 cup (60 ml) fresh or frozen blueberries
A few sprigs fresh parsley
2 tsp dried red algae
4 tsp standardized ginkgo biloba extract

In a blender, purée orange juice, carrot, parsley, and blueberries*. Stir in algae and ginkgo biloba. Drink 1 glass every morning for 3 weeks, every 2 months.

* A juicer can also be used for this step.

Extremely rich in flavonoids (vitamin PP) and carotenoids, red algae is a remarkable circulation booster and is considered one of the most effective plants for relieving the symptoms of "heavy legs" syndrome, strengthening weak capillaries, and treating varicose veins. Ginkgo biloba extract improves circulation to the lower limbs by promoting blood vessel dilation.

Green Tea and Kiwi

1 serving

2 kiwis, peeled
1/3 cup (80 ml) green tea (Kukicha or sencha), chilled*
Juice of **1** lemon
1 tsp cane syrup
Crushed ice

* To prepare green tea, infuse 1-1/2 tsp Kukicha tea leaves in 2/3 cup (160 ml) boiling water. Use 1/3 cup (80 ml) of the chilled tea in your smoothie.

In a blender, purée all ingredients until smooth. Drink immediately.

The tannins in green tea help burn fat, while the polyphenols it contains lower blood sugar levels by dissolving unhealthy triglycerides. Caffeine also helps the body burn more calories, and has a diuretic effect. Besides water, tea is the only naturally calorie-free beverage.

Smoothies for Weight Loss

Smoothies are a valuable addition to any weight loss plan. If made with the right healthy ingredients, they are a delicious source of energy that is low in calories and high in vitamins, minerals, and fiber. To make a great weight loss smoothie, it is important to choose fruits with a low glycemic index, such as citrus fruits, peaches, apples, pears, strawberries, and raspberries. The body digests these fruits more slowly, which in turn slows the absorption of sugar into the bloodstream, preventing the body from converting excess glucose into stored fat. A low glycemic index also helps the body feel full longer.

Exotic Fruit Smoothie (Meal Replacement)

3 servings

2 tbsp coconut milk
1 cup (250 ml) orange juice
1 cup (250 ml) soft tofu, drained
1/2 fresh or frozen banana
1/2 fresh pineapple, peeled and cut into pieces

In a blender, purée all ingredients until smooth. Serve.

Variation: Use soy milk instead of orange juice, and if you don't like pineapple, replace it with 1 cup (250 ml) fresh or frozen mango.

Soft tofu, also known as silken tofu, should be stored in water and will keep in the refrigerator for 7 to 10 days. Change the tofu water daily.

Drink a tasty smoothie for breakfast to jump-start your day, and for an extra energy boost, pair it with a slice of whole-wheat toast and a few fresh-cut raw veggies.

Strawberry Cantaloupe

2 servings

1 **cup (250 ml)** orange juice
1/2 cantaloupe, cut into pieces
1/2 fresh or frozen banana
10 fresh or frozen strawberries
1/2 **cup (125 ml)** fat-free Greek yogurt
2 tsp honey

In a blender, or with a hand blender, purée all ingredients until smooth. If the mixture is too thick, add a bit of orange juice. Serve.

Juicy and refreshing, cantaloupe is known for its high concentration of provitamin A (carotene) and as a good source of vitamin C. It is also low in calories and contains fiber, which gives it a mild laxative effect.

Berries and Tofu
(Meal Replacement)

1 serving

1/2 **cup (125 ml)** grape juice
1-1/2 cups (375 ml) fresh or frozen blackberries, strawberries, raspberries, and/or blueberries
1/2 fresh or frozen banana
1/2 **cup (125 ml)** soft tofu, drained
1 tbsp cane syrup

In a blender, purée all ingredients until smooth. If the mixture is too thick, add a bit of grape juice or soy milk.

Soft tofu, also known as silken tofu, should be stored in water and will keep in the refrigerator for 7 to 10 days. Change the tofu water daily.

Eating tofu is a great way to benefit from the health-giving properties of soy — it is high in protein and cholesterol free. Drink this smoothie as an energy-boosting meal replacement!

Health Break

1/2 cup (125 ml) 1% milk
2 tbsp fat-free yogurt
1/2 cup (125 ml) fresh or frozen raspberries
1 tsp agave syrup
1 tbsp psyllium

In a blender, or with a hand blender, purée all ingredients until smooth. Drink immediately.

Psyllium is composed mainly of hemicellulose, a fiber that acts like a sponge by absorbing liquid in the digestive tract. It can help you lose weight by providing a feeling of fullness, which reduces the appetite; it also stimulates peristalsis, the passage of food through the digestive system. Getting enough dairy can also help speed up the weight loss process; the recommended daily intake of dairy products for adults is two servings a day.

Slimming Peach

1 cup (250 ml) rice milk
1 cup (250 ml) fresh or frozen peaches, cut into pieces
2 tbsp almond butter

In a blender, or with a hand blender, purée all ingredients until smooth. Drink immediately.

Peaches are composed mainly of water, so they are thirst quenching and rehydrating. They also contain provitamin A, an antioxidant, and they help stimulate the excretory system thanks to their high fiber content.

Fig and Pear

1 serving

3 or 4 fresh figs
1 or 2 pears, peeled, cored, and cut into pieces
1/2 cup (125 ml) fat-free Greek yogurt

In a blender, or with a hand blender, purée all ingredients until smooth. If the mixture is too thick, add a bit of 1% milk.

One fresh fig has about 25 calories — a tasty (and elegant!) dessert to include in any weight loss plan. This fiber-rich fruit is highly recommended for frequent constipation sufferers, and contains various minerals, B vitamins, and anthocyanins, which play a vital role in maintaining blood vessel health. Pears, for their part, are low in calories, have a high water content, and surpass most other foods in their level of folate, which supports neuromuscular function.

The Big Bran

1 red apple, unpeeled, cored, and quartered
1 cup (250 ml) fresh or frozen strawberries
1 cup (250 ml) watermelon
2 tbsp oat or wheat bran
2 tbsp flaxseeds
Crushed ice

In a blender, or with a hand blender, purée all ingredients until smooth. If using fresh berries and crushed ice, use a blender. If the mixture is too thick, add a bit of water.

Variation: Use raspberries, if you prefer. This smoothie is just ever so slightly sweet, but incredibly rich in fiber, vitamins, and omega-3 fatty acids, thanks to the flaxseeds it contains. Oat bran is an ally in weight loss that, while promoting healthy digestion, limits calorie absorption from the food being digested. It also helps prevent the onset of diabetes, reduces the risk of colon cancer, and lowers cholesterol levels.

Smoothies for Sport

The key to an active lifestyle is a balanced diet that provides all of your essential nutrients, adapted not only to the sport, but also to the time of day the sport is being practised. When the muscles are working, they use up energy, and the two main sources of fuel for muscles are carbohydrates (sugars) and fat. Simple carbohydrates include sugar and fruit juice; complex carbohydrates include oatmeal and whole grains. Smoothies are nutritious and quick to make, and can often replace a meal.

Wake-Up Smoothie

1 serving

1 cup (250 ml) soy milk
1 banana
1 orange
10 to **15** fresh or frozen raspberries or strawberries
1 tsp fresh ginger, grated
Crushed ice

In a blender, purée all ingredients until smooth. Serve immediately.

This smoothie is rich in vitamin C. Drink one per day for two weeks, for breakfast, or as a snack.

Kiwi Spirulina Smoothie

1 serving

Juice of **1** orange
1/2 fresh or frozen banana
2 kiwis, peeled
2 tbsp fat-free yogurt (Balkan-style)
1 tsp powdered spirulina

In a blender, purée all ingredients until smooth. If the mixture is too thick, add a bit of milk.

Variation: If desired, replace the kiwis with 1 cup of fresh or frozen berries.

This nutritious smoothie is perfect for people who lead an active lifestyle. Spirulina is high in iron, and the fruit provides vitamin C, which helps the body absorb the iron.

Wake-Up Smoothie

1, 2, 3, Go!

1, 2, 3, Go!

1/4 cup (60 ml) soy milk
1/4 cup (60 ml) orange juice
1/2 cup (125 ml) fresh pineapple, peeled and chopped
1/2 fresh or frozen banana
1/2 cup (125 ml) fresh or frozen mango
1/2 cup (125 ml) soft tofu
1 tbsp partly skimmed powdered milk

In a blender, or with a hand blender, purée ingredients until smooth. Serve immediately.

Soft tofu, also known as silken tofu, should be stored in water and will keep in the refrigerator for 7 to 10 days. Change the tofu water daily.

After exercising, it is important to eat foods containing protein, like milk, tofu, or other soy products. These foods also contain vitamins and calcium, which are absorbed slowly by the body, helping to provide energy.

Restoration Smoothie

1 serving

1 cup (250 ml) 2% milk
1 mango, cut into pieces
1 passion fruit, seeds only
Juice of 1 lime
1 tsp flaxseed oil

In a blender, purée all ingredients until smooth. Drink immediately.

This smoothie helps the body recover after intense physical activity. The betacarotene and the vitamin C in the mango help muscles recuperate, and the magnesium in the passion fruit seeds strengthens the muscles. Flaxseed oil reduces inflammation, and the lime contains vitamin C, which boosts collagen production.

Smoothies for Kids

Studies have shown that visually appealing food affects our perception of taste: if the food looks good, it must taste good, too. Children are particularly sensitive to the way food looks, especially when it comes to fruits and vegetables! Homemade smoothies make an ideal breakfast for kids, especially when they include a source of protein, like tofu or peanut butter, and are delicious as a snack or dessert. Let your imagination run wild and use whatever fruit you have on hand: strawberries, mangoes, kiwis, bananas, pears, blueberries, raspberries, or any fruit of your choice! In winter, frozen berries are an excellent alternative to fresh berries, which are often expensive or unavailable. You have to be creative when it comes to feeding kids, and smoothies are one of the best ways to incorporate vegetables into your child's diet to make sure they get their five to ten servings a day.

Peanut Butter and Banana

1 serving

1 cup (250 ml) whole milk
1 frozen banana
1 tbsp creamy peanut butter

In a blender, or with a hand blender, purée all ingredients until smooth. Serve immediately.

As long as your child is not allergic to peanuts, this quick and easy breakfast smoothie will start the day off on the right foot and only requires a few simple ingredients! The peanut is actually a legume, not a nut, belonging to the same family as the peas and beans we grow in the garden. Peanut butter is a great way to incorporate protein and healthy fat into your child's breakfast, and one tablespoon has just 85 calories, most of which come from healthy fat, protein, and carbohydrates that the body needs to provide energy throughout the day.

Strawberry Mango Morning

1 serving

1/2 cup (125 ml) mango juice
1/2 cup (125 ml) fresh or frozen strawberries
1/2 fresh or frozen banana
1 tbsp lime juice
1/2 cup (125 ml) plain yogurt (Balkan-style)
Crushed ice

In a blender, purée all ingredients until smooth. Serve immediately.

For kids, breakfast is the most important meal of the day. As soon as they wake up, they need to refuel their brains and bodies to prepare for the big day ahead. A complete breakfast keeps energy levels up until lunchtime, helping them maintain their concentration and attention, and avoid that midmorning slump. This smoothie contains plenty of vitamin C and calcium, which, combined with wholegrain cereal, bread, or oatmeal, will provide energy throughout the day.

Pineapple Basil

1/2 cup (125 ml) water
1 cup (250 ml) fresh pineapple, peeled and chopped
1/2 cup (125 ml) fresh basil leaves
1 cup (250 ml) baby spinach
1/2 small banana

In a blender, or with a hand blender, purée all ingredients until smooth. Add a bit of water, if desired. Serve.

Many kids turn their noses up at fruits and veggies, but this smoothie's refreshing flavor will change their minds! Pineapple adds that sweetness they love, along with plenty of vitamins, and the basil gives it a lemony kick and provides vitamin A, calcium, and phosphorus. Spinach, as everyone knows, is rich in potassium, iron, and fiber.

Clementine Smoothie

1 serving

1/2 fresh or frozen banana
10 green grapes
2 clementines, pith removed
1/2 cup (125 ml) plain yogurt (Balkan-style)

In a blender, or with a hand blender, purée all ingredients until smooth. Serve immediately.

Clementines are high in vitamin C, and eating just two a day fulfills half of the recommended daily intake, and provides carotene and vitamin E, which, together with the vitamin C, create the ultimate antioxidant trifecta! Clementines also contain various pigments (flavonoids, anthocyanins, xantophylls) that boost the effects of the vitamin C and strengthen the capillaries. A clementine smoothie paired with a slice of whole-wheat toast is the perfect way to start your day!

Creamy Berry and Bran

1 serving

1/4 cup (60 ml) fresh red berries (strawberries, raspberries)

1/2 cup (125 ml) whole milk

1 tsp honey

1 tsp oat bran

In a blender, or with a hand blender, combine berries, milk, and honey. Add oat bran and let sit for 1 or 2 minutes. Blend again and serve immediately.

This breakfast is a real winner! It is quick and easy to make, and combines a quartet of fortifying foods: milk to promote healthy bones; fruit to provide essential vitamins; honey for energy; and oat bran as a source of fiber. Add a bowl of cereal or a muffin for an energizing morning meal the kids will love!

Express Smoothies

No time to cook breakfast in the morning? No problem! A delicious, nutritious, protein-packed smoothie will help start your day off on the right foot. Quick to make, smoothies are an ideal snack or light meal for the time-pressed gourmet, and an easy way to include a few of the five to ten recommended servings of fruits and vegetables in your diet.

Banana, Plum and Grape

1 serving

1/2 cup (125 ml) orange juice
1/2 banana
1 black plum, pitted
10 to 14 green or red grapes

In a blender, or with a hand blender, purée all ingredients until smooth. Drink immediately.

Cocoberry

2 servings

1/4 cup (60 ml) pear juice
1 cup (250 ml) coconut water
1 cup (250 ml) frozen berries of your choice
1/2 cup (125 ml) yogurt

In a blender, or using a hand blender, purée all ingredients until smooth. Drink immediately.

Express Smoothie

1 serving

1/2 cup (125 ml) plain soy milk
1/4 cup (60 ml) vanilla yogurt
1/4 tsp pure vanilla extract
1/4 cup (60 ml) prunes, pitted and chopped
1/2 frozen banana
Crushed ice

In a blender, purée all ingredients until smooth. Drink immediately.

Banana, Plum and Grape

Breakfast in a Flash

Breakfast in a Flash

2 servings

1/2 cup (125 ml) soy milk
1 apple, left unpeeled, cut into pieces
1/2 cup (125 ml) frozen raspberries
1 cup (250 ml) soft tofu
2 tbsp oat bran
1 tbsp agave syrup

In a blender, or with a hand blender, purée all ingredients until smooth. Drink immediately.

Watermelon Cherry

2 servings

1-1/2 cups (375 ml) watermelon, seeded and cubed
1 cup (250 ml) fresh or frozen cherries, pitted
Juice of 1 lemon
1/2 fresh or frozen banana
15 to 20 fresh mint leaves

In a blender, or with a hand blender, purée all ingredients until smooth and foamy. Chill in the refrigerator before serving.